THE CURIOUS INCIDENT OF THE DOG IN THE NIGHT-TIME

Mark Haddon

SPARK PUBLISHING

SPARKNOTES is a registered trademark of SparkNotes LLC

Spark Publishing
A Division of Barnes & Noble
120 Fifth Avenue
New York, NY 10011
www.sparknotes.com

ISBN: 978-1-4114-7100-9

Please submit changes or report errors to www.sparknotes.com/errors.

Printed in Canada

10 9 8 7 6 5 4

CONTENTS

CONTEXT

MARK HADDON WAS BORN IN NORTHAMPTON, England, in 1962. He graduated from Merton College, Oxford, in 1981, and later returned to his studies at Edinburgh University, where he received a master's degree in English literature. After college, Haddon took a number of odd jobs, including one working with children who had physical and mental disabilities, including autism. He also worked as an illustrator and cartoonist, contributing to a number of prominent British publications. In 1987, Haddon published his first book, *Gilbert's Gobstopper*, about a piece of candy that, over the course of fifty years, gets bounced around the world until it returns to Gilbert, the boy that dropped it (he is an old man by the time it returns). Haddon followed with more than a dozen works for children over the years, many of which he also illustrated, and became involved in writing for children's television. For the British children's show, *Microsoap*, in particular, Haddon won multiple awards, including the Royal Television Society's honor for Best Children's Drama.

In 2003, Haddon published *The Curious Incident of the Dog in the Night-Time*, his first foray into adult fiction. The book follows Christopher John Francis Boone, a young boy whose symptoms and behavior suggest he has a mild form of autism, perhaps Asperger's Syndrome. The book came out in England in two imprints, one aimed at young adults and one at adults, though no differences separated the two editions other than a slight change in the cover artwork. Haddon's novel immediately won fans in each group, quickly selling more than a million copies in both markets, in no small part because of the unique voice of its narrator. The book earned critical acclaim as well, receiving praise from outlets like the *The New York Times* and from noted authors including Ian McEwan. To date, *The Curious Incident of the Dog in the Night-Time* has been published in more than thirty-five countries and has become an international bestseller. In the United Kingdom, Haddon's book has sold more than 2.6 million copies, making it the third best-selling book of the decade.

Had *The Curious Incident of the Dog in the Night-Time* come out ten years earlier, it might have had a difficult time finding grown-up readers. In the early 1990s, few novels about young protagonists found success with adults. But the immense popularity of J.K. Rowling's Harry Potter books, and to a lesser degree Phillip Pullman's "His Dark Materials" series, both of which featured young protagonists coming of age against the backdrop of a dramatic storyline, helped change the way audiences received stories about young adults. Both series achieved popular as well as critical success, with Rowling's books in particular among the biggest sellers of all time. Even though Rowling and Pullman wrote their books for younger audiences, while Haddon wrote his for adults, Haddon's novel found the same kind of crossover appeal. Reflecting this success across age groups are the numerous awards the book has won, which include the Whitbread Book of the Year Award, the Guardian Children's Fiction Prize, and the Booktrust Teenage Prize.

Despite his work with autistic children, Haddon staunchly asserts that he is not an authority on autism and claims to have done very little research on the subject before writing the novel. In an interview with Powell's Books, Haddon said that when he worked with autistic children, "autism wasn't a term that was even used much at the time, and only in retrospect do I realize that some of the people I worked with had autism, although they had it much more seriously than Christopher does." Although the novel never mentions autism, Christopher, the novel's protagonist, displays several of the symptoms that characterize the disorder, such as difficulty reading facial expressions, preoccupation with certain topics, and behaviors like rocking back and forth. Additionally, many of the press releases put out by the publisher, as well as the packaging of certain editions of the book, describe Christopher as autistic. The autistic community has criticized the book for offering an inaccurate depiction of the condition. Haddon, however, says he intended his book only as a work of fiction and not a medical treatise on living with autism.

Plot Overview

The Curious Incident of the Dog in the Night-Time takes place in the year 1998 in and around the town of Swindon, England. The fifteen-year-old narrator of the story, Christopher John Francis Boone, discovers the slain body of his neighbor's poodle, Wellington, on the neighbor's front lawn one evening and sets out to uncover the murderer. His investigation is at times aided, and at other times hampered, by the mild form of autism he lives with. After Christopher hits a policeman in a misunderstanding at the scene of the crime, the police take Christopher into custody. They release him with only a stern warning, on the condition that he promises them and his father not to look into the murder any further.

Christopher chronicles his investigation in a book—the book we are reading—as part of a school assignment. Ignoring repeated warnings from his father, Christopher investigates the crime scene and conducts interviews with the residents of his block. He uncovers a more tangled plot than was first apparent when he discovers that his father and the owner of the slain dog, Mrs. Shears, had a romantic affair. He subsequently learns that their affair began in reaction to another relationship, one carried on between Mr. Shears and Christopher's mother, before she disappeared from Christopher's life.

At school, Christopher prepares for an A-level math exam that will enable him to attend college, a feat no other student at his school has managed. He also continues to work on his book. Upon returning home one afternoon, Christopher accidentally leaves his book in plain view on the kitchen table. His father reads it, becomes angry, and confiscates it. Later, Christopher searches for the book and uncovers a series of letters, hidden in a shirt box in his father's closet, addressed to him from his supposedly dead mother. The letters chronicle the life that his mother has continued to lead with Mr. Shears in London and contain repeated requests for Christopher to respond. In shock, Christopher passes out in his bedroom surrounded by the evidence of his father's deception. When Christopher's father comes home and realizes what has happened, he breaks down in tears. He apologizes for his lies, explaining that he acted out of a desire to protect Christopher from the knowledge of his mother's abandonment of the family.

Christopher's father also admits to killing Wellington after an argument with Mrs. Shears, his lover.

Christopher, now terrified of his father and feeling he can no longer trust him, sneaks out of the house and travels to London to live with his mother. During a harrowing journey, he copes with and overcomes the social fears and limitations of his condition, dodges police, and almost gets hit by a train. His arrival at his mother's flat comes as a total surprise to her, as she had no idea that Christopher's father had been withholding her letters. Christopher settles in for a time at his mother and Mr. Shears's flat, but friction caused by his presence shortly results in his mother's decision to leave Mr. Shears to return to Swindon. Christopher moves into a new apartment with his mother and begins to receive regular visits from his father. When Christopher's pet rat, Toby, dies, Christopher's father gives Christopher a puppy. At school, Christopher sits for his A-level math exam and receives an A grade, the best possible score. The novel ends with Christopher planning to take more A-level exams in physics and advanced math and then attend college in another town. He knows that he can do all of this because he solved the mystery of Wellington's murder, was brave enough to find his mother, and wrote the book that we have read.

CHARACTER LIST

Christopher John Francis Boone The narrator and protagonist of the novel. Fifteen-year-old Christopher is mathematically gifted, yet struggles for social acceptance and understanding as a result of his apparent autism. He views the world largely in absolutes, dividing his life experiences into a series of extreme likes and dislikes. He feels most comfortable with logic and order, making Wellington's murder an irresistible puzzle for him to solve. He resides with his father and pet rat, Toby, at 36 Randolph Street.

Christopher's father (Ed Boone) Single father of Christopher. Father prepares meals for Christopher and sees to his daily needs. Later on, Christopher uncovers elements of Father's life that Father has long tried to keep hidden. Father owns a heating maintenance and boiler repair business.

Christopher's mother (Judy Boone) Christopher believes she died of a heart attack prior to the time when the novel begins. Remembered as a loving but impatient and volatile woman, she was at times overwhelmed by the difficulty of caring for her troubled son.

Mrs. Shears (Eileen Shears) A neighbor of the Boones's. Eileen Shears is the ex-wife of Roger Shears. Christopher remembers that she would often visit to cook meals and play Scrabble after his mother's death. The murder of her dog, Wellington, provides the major dramatic impetus for the novel.

Mr. Shears (Roger Shears) Estranged husband of Eileen Shears. Roger Shears once worked at a bank in town, but moved to London rather suddenly a couple of years earlier, leaving Mrs. Shears behind. His mysterious nature leads Christopher to investigate him as a possible suspect in Wellington's murder.

CHARACTER LIST

Siobhan   Christopher's primary teacher at school. An even-handed mentor, she works to expand Christopher's horizons socially as well as academically. As a result, she is one of the few people whom Christopher trusts, and in the limited moments when the reader sees her, she mirrors the reader as an observer and commentator on Christopher's life.

Mrs. Alexander An elderly resident of Randolph Street. A kind lady, Mrs. Alexander lives a quiet existence filled by caring for her garden and pet dachshund, Ivor. She exhibits grandmotherly tendencies toward Christopher, owing in part to his resemblance to her own grandson. She reveals to Christopher important information about the affairs of Christopher's father and mother.

Wellington Mrs. Shears's large black poodle. Largely docile until an operation left him erratic and occasionally violent, he is found dead in the opening scene of the novel with a garden fork through his side.

Toby   Christopher's brown-and-white pet rat. Christopher adores Toby and treats him as a friend and family member. He later becomes Christopher's sole companion on his harrowing journey to London.

Mr. Jeavons A middle-aged man and the psychologist at Christopher's school.

Rhodri   Father's co-worker. Rhodri is a smelly and obnoxious man who often prods Christopher with difficult math problems for his own amusement, but he also happens to be one of Father's only social outlets.

Julie   Christopher's first primary teacher at school.

Uncle Terry The brother of Ed Boone. He works at a factory in Sunderland.

Reverend Peters Mrs. Peters's husband. A vicar, he agrees to be the invigilator (proctor) for Christopher's A-level math exam, and so plays a key role in determining Christopher's future.

Mrs. Gascoyne Christopher's school principal. Although skeptical of Christopher's abilities, she agrees to let Christopher take his A-level math exam.

Mr. Thompson Resident of Randolph Street. Mr. Thompson is one of the many neighbors whom Christopher interviews during the course of his investigation.

Mr. Wise Another resident on Christopher's block. Another interviewee, he lives with and cares for his disabled mother.

CHARACTER LIST

ANALYSIS OF MAJOR CHARACTERS

CHARACTER ANALYSIS

CHRISTOPHER JOHN FRANCIS BOONE

Christopher's defining characteristic is his inability to imagine the thoughts and feelings of other people. In other words, he cannot empathize. Because he cannot imagine what another person is feeling, he cannot tell when a person speaks sarcastically, or determine a person's mood by his facial expression. This inability to empathize is one of the most prominent features of autism-related disorders, and this characteristic as well as a few others—Christopher's difficulty understanding metaphors, his fixation with certain topics, and his computerlike ability with numbers—strongly suggest that Christopher has a mild form of autism. For Christopher, this condition has made him extraordinarily gifted in math and science but severely underequipped socially, leading Christopher to frequently misunderstand other people, especially his father. As a result, he greatly dislikes social interaction and avoids it when possible.

Although Christopher does not mention autism by name anywhere in the novel, we see that he recognizes the ways he differs from most people and feels keenly aware of these differences. He says, for instance, that although most people enjoy chatting, he hates it because he finds it pointless. He doesn't see social interaction as an end in itself. Thus talking to another person about an unimportant topic serves no purpose. He lives as an outsider as a result. He has very few friends and doesn't trust other people. He feels content to read in his room by himself and he even fantasizes about being the only person alive on the planet. Christopher also recognizes and takes pride in the strengths that result from his condition, such as his talent for math and his remarkably accurate memory. His memory allows him to recall an entire event in extraordinary detail, and he uses it to navigate social interactions by memorizing a chart of facial expressions and the emotions associated with them.

Christopher shows a growing desire for independence throughout the novel, and through much of the novel we watch as Christopher gains the confidence to assert himself. He shows his yearning for independence in a few ways, rebelling against his father by disobeying his orders, for instance, and fantasizing about doing whatever he likes and taking care of himself in his recurring dream of being one of the few people left on Earth. He also begins planning to go to college and to live on his own there. As Christopher overcomes the various trials he faces, he gains confidence in his abilities and gradually becomes more self-sufficient. This process culminates in a difficult journey to London that Christopher undertakes by himself, a feat that represents a significant triumph for him since he has never traveled alone. At the end of the novel, Christopher recognizes that he has overcome his challenges and he feels ready to be on his own.

CHRISTOPHER'S FATHER (ED BOONE)

Christopher's father often goes to extremes when demonstrating his emotions, occasionally blowing up in anger, and he lacks the confidence to work through his problems verbally. When trying to explain himself he stutters and stops and often has trouble connecting sentences. Like Christopher, he has very few friends—Rhodri is the only one the novel mentions. He also feels emotionally devastated by the way his relationship with his wife (Christopher's mother) ended two years earlier, and because he has no one to help him cope with his emotions, he bottles them up until he explodes in anger during stressful situations.

Christopher's father lovingly and diligently cares for Christopher, yet he also struggles with the frustration he feels as a result of not always being able to understand Christopher's behavior. He carefully prepares all of Christopher's meals according to Christopher's rigid list of likes and dislikes, but he also becomes angry with Christopher when Christopher misunderstands him. Notably, he is extremely protective of Christopher. This impulse to protect Christopher and his desire to punish Christopher's mother for the way she left leads him to lie about Mother's leaving. As Christopher discovers more and more of the truth about his mother, his father can see his relationship with Christopher deteriorating. Christopher's father must work to regain his son's trust, and the novel's final chapters focus on his efforts to reestablish a relationship with Christopher.

CHRISTOPHER'S MOTHER (JUDY BOONE)

For the majority of the novel, our only view of Christopher's mother comes through Christopher's memories. He remembers her as loving but impatient and prone to breakdowns in the face of his tantrums. She also comes across as a dreamer who is unable to cope with the harsh realities of Christopher's condition. But she receives a momentary turn as the narrator—the only instance in the novel when the reader sees a first-person point of view other than Christopher's—when Christopher includes in his book a series of her letters in full. In these letters, she exhibits the patience that she lacked in her face-to-face interactions with him, writing forty-three letters over the course of two years, despite getting no response. Although she tells Christopher in the letters that she left him and his father because she thought they would be happier without her, this explanation is clearly only part of her reasoning. We also see in the letters the intense frustration she felt with Christopher and her inability to deal with his behavior, as when Christopher threw a tantrum in a department store while he and his mother were Christmas shopping. She felt unable to cope with these fits of Christopher's, possibly because of her depression, which Christopher mentions at one point in passing. When we finally meet her in person, however, Christopher's mother turns out to be strong-willed and independent. Even so, she evidently still finds dealing with Christopher extremely difficult because of his needs and sometimes inappropriate behavior. She clearly loves Christopher but also has doubts about her ability to take care of him.

Themes, Motifs & Symbols

Themes

The Struggle to Become Independent

Christopher's goal in the novel resembles that of many teenage protagonists in coming-of-age stories: to become independent and find his role in the world. Because of his condition, Christopher cannot be as independent as he would like. Since he has trouble understanding other people, dealing with new environments, and making decisions when confronted with an overload of new information, he has difficulty going places by himself. When he feels frightened or overwhelmed, he has a tendency to essentially shut down, curling himself into a ball and trying to block out the world around him. Christopher, however, still has the typical teenage desire to do what he wants and take care of himself without anyone else telling him what to do. As a result, we see him rebelling against his father in the novel by lying and disobeying his father's orders. We also see this desire for independence in Christopher's dream of being one of the few people left on Earth when no authority figures are present, and in his planning for college, where he wants to live by himself.

Christopher's struggle to become independent primarily involves gaining the self-confidence needed to do things on his own and moving beyond his very rigidly defined comfort zone. Solving Wellington's murder figures into his efforts to be independent in that it forces Christopher to speak with a number of people he doesn't know, which he finds uncomfortable, and it gives him confidence in his ability to solve problems on his own. The A-level math test also represents an avenue to independence for Christopher. By doing well on the test, Christopher can use the test to get into college, allowing him to live on his own. Finally, Christopher's harrowing trip to London serves as his greatest step toward independence. The trip epitomizes everything Christopher finds distressing about the world, such as dealing with social interactions, navigating new environments, and feeling overloaded with information. By overcoming these obstacles, he gains confidence in his ability to face any challenge on his own.

SUBJECTIVITY

Christopher's condition causes him to see the world in an uncommon way, and much of the novel allows the reader to share Christopher's unique perspective. For instance, although the novel is a murder mystery, roughly half the chapters in the book digress from this main plot to give us Christopher's thoughts or feelings on a particular subject, such as physics or the supernatural. To take one example, he tells us about the trouble he has recognizing facial expressions and the difficulty he had as a child understanding how other people respond to a given situation, explaining his preference for being alone that we see throughout the novel. As the story progresses, the book gradually departs from the murder-mystery plot and focuses more on Christopher's character, specifically his reaction to the revelation that his mother did not die but rather left the family to live with another man while his father lied about the situation. Throughout these events, the reader typically understands more about Christopher's situation than Christopher does. When Christopher discovers the letters from his mother hidden in his father's closet, for example, Christopher invents different reasons to explain why a letter from his mother would be dated after her supposed death. The reader, on the other hand, may recognize immediately that his mother did not die and that Christopher's father has been lying to him.

Although the reader recognizes that Christopher has an uncommon perspective of the world, the novel suggests that everyone, in fact, has a subjective point of view. By giving detailed explanations of Christopher's thoughts, the novel allows the reader to empathize with Christopher. Moreover, by pointing out the irrational behaviors of so-called normal people, such as Christopher's father's habit of putting his pants on before his socks, the novel implies that Christopher's eccentricities are actually typical to a degree. As a result, the reader is able to take on Christopher's perspective as his own and to understand Christopher's reasons for behaving as he does. Christopher's point of view loses its strangeness and seems merely unique.

THE DISORDER OF LIFE

Christopher has an urgent need to see the world as orderly, and he has a very low tolerance for disorder. He obsesses over schedules, for instance, and even describes the difficulty he had going on vacation with his parents because they had no routine to follow. Moreover, because Christopher has such difficulty connecting to people on an emotional level, he relies heavily on order and logic to understand and navigate the world. The narration, as a result, frequently veers away from the main storyline to discuss topics, such as physics or even the rate of growth of a pond's frog population, that have clearly defined and logical rules. When the narration moves back to Christopher's life, the messiness of the social and emotional lives of Christopher and those around him becomes even more apparent.

Over the course of the novel, Christopher experiences a series of increasingly destabilizing events, such as learning of Mother's affair and Father's deceptions, revealing that Christopher's narrow focus on order at the beginning of the novel actually keeps him— and the reader—blind to the complex tangle of relationships within his family. This disorder grows increasingly prominent as the story progresses. When Christopher leaves Swindon to find his mother in London, he becomes literally paralyzed at times by the disorder of the massive urban landscape he passes through, which symbolizes the disorder he faces in his family. The novel concludes with the various characters resolving some of their issues, but with their lives remaining essentially as untidy as ever.

THEMES

COPING WITH LOSS

Each of the major characters endures his share of loss in *The Curious Incident of the Dog in the Night-Time*. The novel opens with a death: Wellington's murder, which prompts Christopher to think back on an earlier moment of loss in his life—the death of his mother. At the time, he coped with his mother's death by accepting that his mother was gone and moving on, in spite of the fact that he could not say good-bye before she passed. Later, he often remembers her in his writing, sharing detailed memories of her manner of speaking, dress, and temperament. Father also copes with the loss of his wife, Christopher's mother, though he does so by breaking off contact with her and cutting her out of his—and Christopher's—life, telling Christopher she is dead. Father's feelings of loss arise again when Mrs. Shears ends their relationship, and he works through his loss violently by murdering Wellington, effectively setting the events of the novel in motion. Ultimately, the book ends as it began, with a death, this time of Christopher's pet rat, Toby. Christopher copes by acknowledging that Toby lived a very long life for a rat, and he rejoices in the arrival of a new puppy, Sandy.

MOTIFS

FRUSTRATION WITH CHRISTOPHER

Many of the characters in the novel become irritated with Christopher at one time or another because of the difficulty they have communicating with him. Christopher has trouble understanding metaphors, such as *the dog was stone dead*. He also has difficulty with nonverbal forms of communication, such as body language, facial expressions, and even the tone of someone's voice. He tends to take statements literally and requires very specific instructions in order to follow a command. He says, for example, that when people say "Be quiet" they don't specify how long he should be quiet for. As a result, we often see characters struggling to make Christopher understand them since their ordinary way of speaking fails to communicate their meaning to him. These exchanges underscore how Christopher's condition affects his social skills, and they emphasize for the reader the difference in perspective that Christopher experiences compared to the average person.

SCIENCE AND TECHNOLOGY

Christopher's frequent asides about science and technology, such as his fantasies of astronauts and space shuttles and musings about alien life forms and the workings of the human mind, recur throughout the book. Christopher feels most comfortable with subjects that he views as logical, such as physics and math. As a result, he thinks about these topics continually. But Christopher also displays a fascination with subjects that appear to him vastly greater in scope than human life, such as the relationship between time and space or the nature of stars, which he breathlessly describes as "the very molecules of life." These subjects appear to allow Christopher to put his own life in perspective, helping him to cope with the difficulties he encounters on a daily basis.

ANIMALS

Christopher often finds solace in interacting with animals and displays great consternation when he sees them harmed. He engages with animals so readily because he finds them easier to understand than people. An animal expresses its wants and needs plainly. Dogs, for example, growl when they feel threatened and wag their tails when they feel happy. Christopher can understand these simple visual cues. He even praises the nature of dogs early in the novel, saying they're faithful and honest and more interesting than some people. Consequently, animals often serve as a foundation for trust between Christopher and other human beings. Christopher speaks with Mrs. Alexander in part because she cares well for her dachshund, Ivor. Later, after Father hits Christopher when he finds the detailed record of Christopher's investigation, he takes Christopher to the Twycross Zoo to apologize, because he understands that Christopher will find the environment comforting. Animals, particularly Toby, Christopher's pet rat, also provide Christopher with the companionship he doesn't find in other people. Toby even serves as Christopher's constant travel companion. When Toby dies, Father buys Christopher a puppy, hoping to rebuild his trust with Christopher and to provide Christopher with a new companion.

SYMBOLS

THE MURDER INVESTIGATION

Christopher's book begins as a mystery novel about the murder of his neighbor's dog, but as Christopher's investigation progresses, it comes to represent Christopher's search for the truth about his mother and father. As Christopher searches for clues about Wellington's murder, he finds evidence revealing that his father has been lying to him about his mother's death. Investigating Wellington's murder becomes an excuse for Christopher to uncover the secrets that Father has kept from him, and Father's deception acts as a crime in itself. Ultimately, we learn that Wellington's murder and Father's deception constitute separate parts of the same investigation. Father lied to Christopher in large part because of the feelings of loss and anger he felt when Christopher's mother left him. When Mrs. Shears broke off her affair with Father, those same lingering feelings of loss and anger caused him to lose control and kill Wellington. Christopher's search for the truth about Wellington essentially leads him to the truth about his mother and father.

LOGIC PUZZLES, MATH PROBLEMS, AND MAPS

Logic puzzles, math problems, and maps symbolize to Christopher the part of the world that is ordered and logical. Accordingly, Christopher uses these items as tools to organize his thinking, like when he uses the so-called Monty Hall problem to explain why his intuition regarding Mr. Shears has been wrong, and they serve as Christopher's primary means of achieving a sense of security. These items recur continually throughout *The Curious Incident of the Dog in the Night-Time*, but they appear most often when Christopher encounters new information that he has not fully processed, or when he experiences a particularly confusing or disturbing event. When his thoughts become jumbled in the train station in Swindon, for instance, Christopher thinks of the visual riddle called Conway's Soldiers to pass the time. He also regularly uses maps to navigate and achieve his goals. He uses a map when he searches the neighborhood for Wellington's murderer, again when he attempts to find the train station in Swindon, and yet again in his effort to find Mother's apartment when he arrives in London. In essence, these different items provide Christopher with a strategy to follow when a problem involves too many variables for him to reach a clear solution.

The A-level Test in Math

For Christopher, the A-level math test represents a way for him to validate himself and feel proud. Because of his condition, Christopher is socially inept and attends a school for children with disabilities. But Christopher does not feel that the other children in the school are really his peers. His condition, while a handicap, doesn't limit him to the extent that the other children's disabilities limit them. Christopher recognizes this fact and also knows that he is exceptionally gifted in math and science, causing him to feel generally superior to his classmates. Christopher, however, seeks to prove this superiority, and the A-level math test gives him the opportunity. His preoccupation with the test in the later sections of the novel shows how much he wants the opportunity to prove his ability.

Summary & Analysis

Chapters 2–41

Summary: Chapter 2

The book opens seven minutes after midnight, when the narrator, Christopher John Francis Boone, finds Wellington, the poodle belonging to Mrs. Shears, his neighbor, dead on Mrs. Shears's lawn with a garden fork through its side. Christopher touches the dog's muzzle and observes that it is still warm. He wonders who killed Wellington, and why.

Summary: Chapter 3

Departing from his story (Christopher does this frequently throughout the novel), Christopher explains that he has difficulty determining people's emotions from their facial expressions. But he can name each country in the world, their capitals, and every prime number up to 7,057. He recalls the first time he met Siobhan, eight years earlier. She drew faces on a piece of paper and asked him what emotions the faces expressed. Christopher could only identify the sad face, which represents how he felt when he found Wellington dead, and the happy face, which shows how he feels when he wanders the neighborhood at three or four in the morning. He could not identify the other emotions.

Summary: Chapter 5

The story returns to Mrs. Shears's lawn, where Christopher removes the garden fork and picks up Wellington. Mrs. Shears appears on her patio and yells at Christopher to get away from her dog. Mrs. Shears does not stop yelling, even when he puts the dog down. So Christopher puts his hands over his ears and curls into a ball on the grass, trying to block out the sound.

Summary: Chapter 7

Christopher reveals that we are reading his murder-mystery novel, written after Siobhan advised him to try writing a story he would want to read. Siobhan thought that the opening of the novel should grab people's attention, which is one of the reasons that Christopher started it with Wellington's death. The other reason is that he could not start it any other way: this story actually happened to him, and he has trouble putting events in any order other than the order in which they occurred.

Summary: Chapter 11

Two police officers arrive at the crime scene. Christopher initially finds their presence comforting, but he grows agitated when one policeman begins to ask him questions too quickly, seeming to implicate him in the murder. Christopher curls into a ball again, and he hits the police officer when the officer tries to lift him to his feet.

Summary: Chapter 13

Christopher states that his book will not be funny. To be funny you have to tell jokes, and jokes often rely on the multiple meanings of words. The fact that one word can have multiple meanings confuses Christopher and makes him uncomfortable, so he will not put jokes in his book.

Summary: Chapter 17

The officer arrests Christopher for assault. As the officer drives him away, Christopher considers the Milky Way through the window of the squad car. He feels comforted by the order he sees in the stars, and by the fact that the policeman has done his job in a predictable manner.

Summary: Chapter 19

Christopher describes the rules used to determine prime numbers, a potentially infinite number of which exist. He thinks prime numbers are like life: logical, but impossible to fully comprehend. He likes them, so he has ordered the chapters in his book according to prime numbers.

Summary: Chapter 23

At the police station, Christopher empties his pockets at the front desk, carefully describing every item. When the police put him in his cell, he marvels that the cell is almost a perfect cube. He wonders if Mrs. Shears lied and told the police that he killed Wellington.

Summary: Chapter 29

Christopher finds people confusing because they often communicate nonverbally through facial expressions. They also use metaphors, which equate one thing with another when neither has any actual relation to the other.

SUMMARY: CHAPTER 31

Father arrives at the station and greets Christopher by holding up his hand with his fingers outspread. Christopher does the same, allowing their fingers to touch. Christopher explains that they greet each other this way because he does not like to be hugged. An officer takes Christopher to the investigator, who releases Christopher with a stern warning.

SUMMARY: CHAPTER 37

Christopher explains that in order to form a lie he would have to pick an event that did not happen to replace the one that did. But he can't pick any one thing from among the infinite number of things that did not happen, so he does not tell lies. Consequently, everything that he has written in his book is true.

SUMMARY: CHAPTER 41

On the drive home, Christopher tries to apologize to his father for making him come to the police station, but his father does not want to talk about it. When they arrive home, Christopher goes to his room. At 2:07 AM he goes to the kitchen to get a drink before bed, and notices his father sitting alone in the living room with tears in his eyes. Christopher asks him if he feels sad about Wellington. His father stares at him for a long time before replying that he does.

ANALYSIS: CHAPTERS 2–41

The book begins unconventionally, starting with chapter 2 instead of chapter 1, and rapidly progresses through the prime numbers until we have finished chapter 41 at the end of the section. Christopher has chosen to write the book this way simply because he prefers prime numbers, with their specificity of pattern, to standard numbers. Christopher also digresses repeatedly from the mystery of Wellington's murder right from the start, veering into discussions of what he knows (countries and their capitals, for example) and the difficulties he has understanding people. The reader can see by this point that, although *The Curious Incident of the Dog in the Night-Time* may use some conventions of murder-mystery narratives, it will hardly be a conventional story in that genre. The ways it diverges from convention, digressing into discussions of numbers for instance, give the reader insight into how Christopher views the world. Specifically, Christopher's observations on prime numbers tell us that Christopher values order and has a gifted mathematical mind.

Christopher has very poor social skills, stemming from his inability to imagine what other people are thinking or feeling, and in this section we already see this limitation playing out in the story. For instance, we see that Christopher is easily misled by lies when Christopher finds his father alone in the living room crying. Father says he feels sad because of Wellington, though the reader recognizes that this excuse is not true. Christopher, who cannot understand that his father is lying, believes him and returns to his room without questioning the matter any further. This difficulty identifying lies makes it all the more extraordinary that Christopher investigates the mystery of Wellington's murder. We also see Christopher's poor social skills at work when he has difficulty explaining himself after Mrs. Shears and the policeman confront him about Wellington. He quickly feels overwhelmed and withdraws into a ball. Repeatedly, Christopher's social deficits lead to misunderstandings and conflicts. For instance, Christopher's inability to explain why he was holding Wellington's body leads Mrs. Shears to think that Christopher killed Wellington. In fact, Christopher's poor social skills play such a prominent role right from the start of the story that the reader can assume they will have greater ramifications later on.

Christopher recognizes his social limitations, and he focuses instead on the extraordinary intelligence he displays in other areas. The main evidence of this intelligence comes from Christopher's ability to deal with concepts that other people find abstract and difficult to comprehend. He clearly and succinctly explains why the Milky Way appears in the sky as it does, for example. He also tells the reader that he can identify all the prime numbers up to 7,057, indicating that he has a particularly savantlike ability with numbers. Christopher compares prime numbers to life, saying that both are logical but that you can never work out the rules, no matter how hard you try. He believes that, like prime numbers, life abides by rules. In other words, he does not see life as random and chaotic, even though he recognizes that he cannot know all its rules. Instead, Christopher knows his strengths and weaknesses and lives contentedly with them.

Christopher's obsession with the physical details of his surroundings, particularly aspects of color, number, and time, serves as a great asset to him in his investigation. Christopher describes scenes in very specific detail. After the police put him in jail, for instance, he comments on the ordered dimensions of his cell before considering why he is in prison in the first place. When the officer makes him turn in his belongings at the police station, he lists in great detail every item in his pockets. This attention to detail helps Christopher to counter the disadvantages he faces from his lack of social skills and allows him to gather clues related to Wellington's murder. He notices that Wellington's muzzle still feels warm when he finds Wellington dead, for instance.

CHAPTERS 43–61

SUMMARY: CHAPTER 43
Christopher remembers the day two years earlier when Mother died. He came home from school and found the house empty. When his father arrived home later, he made several phone calls to locate her and then went out for a few hours. When he returned, he told Christopher that Mother was in the hospital because of a heart problem and that Christopher wouldn't be able to visit. Christopher decided to make her a get-well card, and Father promised to bring it to her the next day.

SUMMARY: CHAPTER 47
The morning after Wellington's murder, Christopher spots four red cars in a row on his bus ride to school, making the day a Good Day. Christopher explains that he ranks the day according to the number and color of the cars he sees on his way to school. Three red cars in a row equal a Good Day, and five equal a Super Good Day. Four yellow cars in a row make it a Black Day. On Black Days Christopher refuses to speak to anyone and sits by himself at lunch. The school psychologist, Mr. Jeavons, points out that Christopher's system surprises him since Christopher is so logical. Christopher says he likes to have an order for things, even if the order isn't logical. He acknowledges it makes him feel safe. He says Father puts his trousers on before his socks every morning because it is his order, not because of logic. Christopher decides that he will set out once more to find Wellington's killer because it is a Good Day.

SUMMARY: CHAPTER 53
Christopher recalls that Mother died two weeks after going into hospital. He never saw her there, but Father said that she sent lots of love and had his get-well card on her bedside table before she had an unexpected heart attack. Her death surprised Christopher because she had lived an active and healthy life and was only thirty-eight years old. On the night she died, Mrs. Shears came over and held

Father against her chest to comfort him. She also cooked dinner, and afterward Christopher beat her in Scrabble.

SUMMARY: CHAPTER 59

Back in the present, Christopher sets out to investigate Wellington's murder. He knocks on Mrs. Shears's door, and when she answers, explains that he did not kill Wellington. Mrs. Shears, however, closes the door in his face. Christopher walks back down the sidewalk, and he can see Mrs. Shears's shadow as she watches him through the frosted glass of her doorway. He waits until she leaves, then sneaks around the side of her house and jumps the garden wall. In the garden he finds a locked shed. He looks through the window of the shed and sees the garden fork used in the murder. Christopher concludes that the murderer had to know Mrs. Shears in order to have access to her garden fork. Just then Mrs. Shears discovers him in her garden and threatens to call the police. Christopher goes home, happy to have discovered a clue.

SUMMARY: CHAPTER 61

Christopher remembers a vicar named Reverend Peters, who said heaven was a different kind of place from our universe. Christopher believes that heaven doesn't exist. He reasons that heaven could possibly lie on the other side of a black hole, but for the dead to get there they'd have to be fired off into space by rocket.

ANALYSIS: CHAPTERS 43–61

Christopher has a strong desire for order, and he works to remove any sense of disorder from his life. For instance, his system for determining how good the day will be, despite its apparent illogicality, provides him with a sense of control over the ambiguities and uncertainties he encounters every day. For similar reasons, Christopher cannot accept the idea of heaven's existence since it violates everything he knows about the universe, meaning if heaven exists the order he knows is wrong. As Christopher admits in his conversation with Mr. Jeavons, order makes him feel safe, even when that order is not logical. Though Christopher justifies the irrational aspects of his need for order, such as using the colors of the cars he sees to forecast whether or not the day will be good, by saying that everyone behaves in this way, it's apparent that Christopher isn't really interested in how logical his system is. He uses it because the sense of order it gives him makes him feel safe.

In his unemotional response to his mother's death, Christopher demonstrates his inability to maintain strong emotional connections and again shows his need for order. While describing his mother's death, Christopher focuses on the mundane details of time and place and he omits any mention of his own emotional response to the tragedy. He does not talk about her subsequent absence from the household, for instance, and the effect it had on him and Father. Although Christopher clearly was fond of his mother, evidenced by his desire to take food to her when she was in the hospital, she essentially ceased to play a role in his life when she disappeared. To cope with that loss, Christopher reordered his life without her in it. His writing betrays how much he continues to think about her, however, as he dedicates three of the five chapters in this section to discussing her death.

Christopher's observations about Father's pain and anger allow him to describe the emotion of an event when he is incapable of, or uninterested in, writing about his own feelings on the subject. Throughout Christopher's memories of his mother's death, the reader can see the pain and anger that Father tries to hide from Christopher. When Mrs. Shears holds Father's head against her bosom on the day that Christopher's mother "dies," we see the emotional toll that the events have had on Father. Whether or not Mother's death had a strong emotional effect on Christopher remains unclear, in large part because Father prevented Christopher from visiting Mother in the hospital. As a result, Christopher has no direct recollection of the experience except for the conversations he had with his father.

CHAPTERS 67–73

SUMMARY: CHAPTER 67
Inspired by his Good Day, Christopher draws a map of his neighborhood and sets out to question the people on his block about the murder. He does not like talking to strangers, so he clutches his Swiss Army knife tightly inside his pocket as he approaches Mr. Thompson's house. Mr. Thompson claims to have been away on the night of the murder. The resident at Number 44 does not have any information. Christopher next tries Number 43, but the occupant jokes about policemen getting younger and younger, and Christopher, who hates being laughed at, walks away. He skips Number 38 because he fears the people who live there. At Number

39, Mrs. Alexander, an elderly neighbor, works in her front garden. She has nothing to add regarding Wellington's murder but invites Christopher in for tea. He refuses to go inside, so Mrs. Alexander decides to bring biscuits out for him. Christopher, however, worries she might be calling the police and walks away.

Christopher has an insight about who might have killed Wellington. He figures there are three reasons someone might kill a dog: because they hate the dog; because they are crazy; or because they want to upset the owner. Christopher cannot think of anyone who hated Wellington and does not know anyone who is crazy. He does know that most murderers know their victim and thinks that the only person who would want to upset Mrs. Shears is Mr. Shears. Mr. Shears left about two years earlier and didn't come back. When Mother died, Mrs. Shears would come over and cook for Christopher and his father because she felt lonely, too. Sometimes she even stayed overnight. Christopher doesn't know why Mr. Shears left Mrs. Shears, but if Mr. Shears didn't want to live in the same house as Mrs. Shears anymore he probably hated her. He might have decided to kill Wellington to make her sad. Christopher decides to find out more about Mr. Shears.

SUMMARY: CHAPTER 71
Christopher considers all of the other children at his school stupid. He knows he should refer to them as "special needs" but finds that term silly because everyone has special needs. Siobhan needs very thick glasses in order to see, and Mrs. Peters has to wear a beige-colored hearing aid in order to hear. Christopher plans to prove that he is not stupid like his peers by scoring an A grade on his A-level math test, which no one at his school has done before. After the A-level math test he will take an even more advanced math test and an advanced physics test, and use his scores to attend college in another town.

SUMMARY: CHAPTER 73
Christopher describes the arguments that his mother and father used to have as so bad that he thought they might get divorced. Their fighting, he says, had to do with the stress that resulted from taking care of him and dealing with his behavioral problems. He recalls that sometimes his behavioral problems would make his mother and father angry at each other. His mother used to say Christopher would lead her to an early grave. He writes that many

of his problems have gone now, because he has grown up and can make decisions for himself.

ANALYSIS: CHAPTERS 67–73

In the course of Christopher's investigation, we see both Christopher's strengths and the disadvantages he faces. Although Christopher gets little useful information out of his neighbors, his analytical skills provide him with a key insight about who killed Wellington. He concludes logically that the murderer most likely knew Wellington beforehand. At the same time, however, Christopher apparently remains blind to the nature of Father's relationship with Mrs. Shears. He recalls that Mr. Shears moved out at roughly the same time that Mother died, so Mrs. Shears would often cook dinner for Christopher and Father because she felt lonely, too. Christopher notes that Mrs. Shears would sometimes stay the night, suggesting she and Father had a sexual relationship. Christopher doesn't recognize this detail, presumably because he doesn't stop to imagine what motivation Mrs. Shears might have for sleeping over when her own bed is just next door. The significance of this relationship remains unclear, but Christopher doesn't even realize it may provide a lead worth looking into.

Although Christopher never displays any guilt over his mother's death, his writing suggests that he may feel responsible for her death (though whether he actually does or not remains uncertain). Notably, Christopher says that the problems caused by his behavioral issues led Mother and Father to fight at times, and he is aware that his actions caused his parents a great deal of stress. Christopher then recalls his mother telling him he would drive her into an early grave. He mentions this detail shortly after talking about how she died surprisingly young. Christopher, however, never stops to reflect on this detail. He avoids his own emotional reaction to this comment, perhaps because he had no reaction or because he feels uncomfortable recalling it, and instead picks up with the events that occurred after he went home from questioning his neighbors. The reader can only guess whether Christopher connects his behavioral problems to Mother's comment and ultimately to her death.

Christopher's feelings about his classmates, which we also see in this section, indirectly disclose his feelings about his own condition. Christopher opens chapter 71 by saying all the other children at his school are "stupid." He admits that he shouldn't call them stupid (though that is what they are, he says). He should call them "special needs." Christopher clearly feels superior to these "special needs" children and displays strong feelings of resentment at having been lumped in with them at his school. He wants to take the A-level math test in part to prove he is smarter than they are. He also takes issue with the term "special needs." Christopher recognizes that he does, in fact, fit into the category of "special needs," but in a sense disarms the term by saying everyone has special needs. As examples, he says Siobhan wears thick glasses because she has special needs regarding her eyesight, and Mrs. Peters wears a hearing aid because she has special needs regarding her hearing. Evidently Christopher recognizes his condition. But he doesn't think that it makes him any less capable than the average person.

CHAPTERS 79–89

SUMMARY: CHAPTER 79
When Christopher gets home, Father has made supper and sits at the table in the kitchen. Father has carefully arranged Christopher's food on his plate so that no food item touches another. Father asks Christopher where he has been. Christopher responds with a white lie—that he has been out—because it is only a partial retelling of the truth, and not made up. Father notes that Mrs. Shears has already called to report that he had been poking around her garden. Christopher explains that he thinks Mr. Shears killed Wellington. At the mention of Mr. Shears, Father bangs the table in anger. He forbids Christopher from ever mentioning Mr. Shears's name again and orders him to stop asking questions about who killed Wellington. Christopher sits in silence for a moment. He promises Father that he will do as Father says.

SUMMARY: CHAPTER 83
Christopher wants to be an astronaut. He explains the many ways the job would suit him: he is intelligent, he understands how machines work, and he doesn't mind small spaces, so long as he doesn't share them with anyone. Besides, no yellow or brown things exist on spaceships, and the stars would surround him. It would be a dream come true.

SUMMARY: CHAPTER 89
At school the next day, Christopher shows Siobhan his "finished" book. Now that he has promised Father not to continue the case, he won't be able to write it anymore. Siobhan says it does not matter,

that he has written a good book and should be proud to have written it. But to Christopher the book lacks an ending. He has not found the murderer, and the idea that the person who killed Wellington could be living somewhere nearby, waiting for him when he goes for a walk at night, bothers him. After all, murderers tend to know their victims.

Christopher tells Siobhan that Father told him never to mention Mr. Shears's name in the house again. Siobhan points out that Mrs. Shears is a friend of Christopher and Father, so perhaps Father doesn't like Mr. Shears because he left Mrs. Shears, which would constitute doing something bad to a friend. Christopher points out that Father said Mrs. Shears isn't a friend anymore either.

The next day Christopher sees four yellow cars in a row on his way to school, making it a Black Day. He doesn't eat anything at lunch and reads by himself in a corner during class. The next day he sees four yellow cars again. On the third day he keeps his eyes closed on the ride to school to avoid another Black Day.

ANALYSIS: CHAPTERS 79–89

Chapter 79 hints at some uncomfortable history between Christopher's father and Mr. Shears that the reader has not learned about. Most notably, we see Christopher's father become angry to the point of a physical outburst when Christopher brings up Mr. Shears at the kitchen table. Although Father seems to be exploding at Christopher mostly as a result of the other pressures in his life, the anger arises specifically at the mention of Mr. Shears. Father then forbids Christopher from speaking of Mr. Shears again and calls Mr. Shears "evil." This strong emotional reaction to Mr. Shears suggests that something occurred in the past that Christopher does not know about at this point, nor does the reader. The fact that Mr. Shears is currently Christopher's prime suspect in Wellington's murder suggests his character may play a more significant role later in the novel. When Father forbids Christopher from inquiring anymore about Wellington, he creates a new conflict for Christopher. He must now decide between obeying his father and doing what he wants.

Although Christopher doesn't say explicitly that his father's anger over Mr. Shears upset him, Christopher feels unhappy for the next two days, suggesting a link between Father's reaction and his emotional state. In his writing, he treats this fact as coincidental. The reason he gives is that each day he saw four yellow cars in a row, which according to his system means the day is going to be a Black Day, as he calls them. But the reader can see that Christopher may also be reacting to his father's anger over both the trouble Christopher has gotten into investigating Wellington's death and his father's apparently troubled history with Mr. Shears. After promising his father he won't mention Mr. Shears again or pursue his investigation, Christopher talks about his desire to be an astronaut, which he fantasizes about mainly because it would allow him to work alone, with only limited contact with other people. In other words, he wouldn't have to deal with the complex human emotions and social interactions, such as his interactions with his father, that he finds so difficult to decipher.

In this section, we also see how flexible Christopher can be with his own rules when it suits him. Christopher tells a white lie, as he puts it, to his father about his whereabouts in the afternoon, for instance, although he professes an inability to lie. He carefully notes to the reader the distinction between a "white lie" and a "lie," the former essentially just omitting details, compared to the latter, which entails making up untrue events. But the distinction centers on Christopher's ability to make events up, not on the fact that a white lie still distorts the truth. Later, Christopher closes his eyes on the way to school to avoid seeing yellow cars, which would mean a third Black Day in a row. These loopholes Christopher finds in his own rules imply that Christopher's need for rigidly defined rules is not as great as he makes it out to be. Although he likes having rules because they prevent uncertainties, such as how he should behave in a given situation, like any teenage boy, Christopher has even more interest in getting what he wants.

Chapters 97–101

Summary: Chapter 97

Five days later, Christopher sees five red cars in a row on his way to school, making the day a Super Good Day. He feels that something special will happen. When he gets home, he goes to the shop at the end of the road to buy candy and runs into Mrs. Alexander from house number 39. Mrs. Alexander asks where he went the other day he saw her. When she brought out the biscuits for him, he was gone. Christopher confesses he was afraid she would call the police because he was poking his nose into other people's business.

Christopher exits the shop and pets Mrs. Alexander's dog, which is tied up. He realizes Father didn't ban him from talking about Mr. Shears outside of the house, so he asks Mrs. Alexander about Mr. Shears. She remarks that Christopher knows why Father doesn't like Mr. Shears much. When Christopher asks if Mr. Shears killed Mother, Mrs. Alexander expresses shock to learn that Mother is dead and assures Christopher that Mr. Shears didn't kill Mother.

Christopher asks Mrs. Alexander why she said he knew why Father didn't like Mr. Shears. Mrs. Alexander reveals that Mr. Shears and Mother had an affair. She explains that Father dislikes Mr. Shears as a result, and that Christopher should not mention Mr. Shears in front of Father. Mrs. Alexander makes Christopher promise not to tell Father about their conversation. Christopher goes home.

Summary: Chapter 101

Christopher tells us that Mr. Jeavons believes Christopher likes math because in math straightforward answers exist for every problem, unlike in life. Christopher disagrees that math problems always have straightforward answers, and uses the Monty Hall problem as proof. In 1990, a reader sent a question to Marilyn vos Savant, a columnist at *Parade* magazine, who had the world's highest IQ. The question asked what to do on a game show in which you try to win a car by picking one of three doors. Two of the doors hide goats, while one hides a car. When you pick a door, the host opens one of the two other doors to show a goat, then gives you a chance to change doors. In her answer, vos Savant said you should always change the door you have picked. After she published her answer, mathematicians and scientists wrote in claiming she was wrong, but in fact the math backs up vos Savant's advice. Christopher thinks the problem shows that intuition can be wrong, and that sometimes numbers are complicated and not straightforward at all.

Analysis: Chapters 97–101

Christopher's search for information about Wellington's murderer inadvertently turns up information about his own family. In fact, chapter 97 marks a pivotal moment in the narrative, as Mrs. Alexander reveals to Christopher that Mr. Shears and Christopher's mother had an affair. The revelation puts into perspective Father's angry outburst in the previous section, and perhaps the earlier incident when Christopher found his father crying after they came back from the police station as well. Christopher's father evidently knew about the affair between Christopher's mother and Mr. Shears, and he still feels angry toward Mr. Shears. Christopher, on the other hand, apparently had no idea. When Mrs. Alexander tells him, he seems shocked and just wants to go home rather than continue with his investigation. Christopher set out to uncover the identity of the person who committed one crime, but instead discovered the truth about his parents and his father's reason for disliking Mr. Shears.

Although Christopher doesn't give much description of his emotional response to this news, he gives some hints about his feelings through his explanation of the Monty Hall problem. In essence, Christopher shows that intuition, which he says is what people use in life to make decisions, can lead a person to the wrong answer. A problem that appears straightforward turns out to be not straightforward at all. Christopher never explicitly connects the Monty Hall problem to Mrs. Alexander's revelation about his mother. But the fact that this seeming digression follows immediately after Christopher's conversation with Mrs. Alexander suggests that Christopher sees a parallel between the two. In other words, Christopher feels his own intuition about Mother was wrong, leaving him confused and uncomfortable.

CHAPTERS 103–109

SUMMARY: CHAPTER 103

Christopher returns home and finds Rhodri, a coworker of Father's, talking with Father. Father asks him what he has been up to, and he responds with another white lie about petting Mrs. Alexander's dog outside the shop. Rhodri asks him to multiply 251 and 864, and Christopher replies with the correct answer: 216,864. Father makes Christopher Gobi Aloo Sag for dinner. Gobi Aloo Sag is yellow, so Christopher puts red food coloring in it before he eats it.

On Siobhan's advice, Christopher includes descriptions of things in his book. He goes out into the garden and sees the clouds, which he describes as looking like fish scales and sand dunes. He spots a particularly large cloud moving slowly on the horizon that looks like an alien spaceship and muses that it could easily be one. Aliens, if they exist, would probably be very different from humans. They could be made of air, like clouds, or just about anything else.

SUMMARY: CHAPTER 107

Christopher describes the plot of his favorite book, *The Hound of the Baskervilles* by Sir Arthur Conan Doyle. In it, Sherlock Holmes and Doctor Watson must solve the murder of Sir Charles Baskerville, a wealthy lord whose family is plagued by a giant supernatural dog known as the Hound of the Baskervilles. The hound supposedly killed an ancestor of the family, Hugo, and the very sight of it now appears to have scared Sir Charles to death. Holmes determines that Stapleton, a neighbor of the family who wants to inherit their property, murdered Sir Charles by creating an illusion of the hound. He brought a giant dog from London, covered it in a ghostly coat of glowing paint, and unleashed it on Sir Charles. Holmes and Watson shoot and kill the dog, and then chase Stapleton into the swamp, where he drowns.

Christopher likes *The Hound of the Baskervilles* because it is a detective story with many clues and red herrings. Red herrings are plot elements that lead the reader to think the story will proceed in one direction when the story actually goes another way. Christopher identifies most with Holmes. Like Holmes, he can focus solely on the task at hand and he is able to notice obvious things that other people do not observe.

SUMMARY: CHAPTER 109

Christopher writes some more of his book and takes it to school the next morning to show Siobhan. After she reads it, Siobhan sits down with Christopher to discuss the conversation he had with Mrs. Alexander. Christopher assures her that he does not feel upset about the affair because his mother is dead and Mr. Shears doesn't live nearby anymore. He thinks to feel sad about something that doesn't exist would be stupid.

ANALYSIS: CHAPTERS 103-109

In this section, Christopher repeatedly considers situations in which things turn out to be different from what they initially appear, suggesting an attempt on his part to come to terms with the news of Mother's affair. In chapter 103, he spends time observing clouds that look like fish scales and sand dunes and speculates that aliens need not look like anything found on Earth. In chapter 107, he relates the plot of *The Hound of the Baskervilles*, praising its expert use of red herrings. Christopher's description of a red herring implies that he recognizes Mr. Shears as a red herring in the plot of his own murder mystery. Mr. Shears, who up to now has been Christopher's prime suspect, would not likely have killed Wellington since he has no reason to feel anger toward Mrs. Shears, though Mrs. Shears has plenty of reason to be angry with him. Christopher notes that in *The Hound of the Baskervilles* even the ghostly "hound" turns out to be a dog covered in glow-in-the-dark paint. Eventually, Christopher appears to accept the affair and move on. In chapter 109, he explains to Siobhan that Mother is dead and Mr. Shears is not around, so dwelling on their affair makes no sense to him. Wellington's murder, on the other hand, remains a mystery he wants to solve.

In this section, we also see that Christopher's admiration of the character of Sherlock Holmes allows him to emphasize the positive aspects of his condition. Christopher, as we've seen throughout the book, recognizes the limits his condition imposes on him, notably his difficulty connecting socially with other people, and he looks for ways to downplay these limits and play up his strengths. Christopher identifies with Holmes because he sees many of Holmes's traits in himself. He feels he shares Holmes's powers of observation and analysis, for instance, which Holmes uses to solve the mysteries he faces. He also sees in himself Holmes's ability to focus entirely on the matter at hand and his strong sense of logic. By praising these attributes in Holmes, Christopher indirectly praises these attributes in himself, boosting his self-esteem and allowing him to overlook the negative aspects of his condition.

Siobhan, meanwhile, plays the role of quiet observer, working much as the reader does to understand Christopher better through his novel. Siobhan initially tells Christopher to write his novel to give him a simple writing exercise, but the book's autobiographical nature soon reveals Christopher's inner thoughts and home life to Siobhan. In chapter 109, Siobhan reads of Mother's affair with Mr. Shears, and she realizes that she has inadvertently learned a secret about Christopher's family. She attempts to engage Christopher in a discussion of his feelings about the affair, but Christopher reveals very little about his emotional reaction, just as he tells the reader little about his feelings on the subject. He instead dismisses the matter with logic, saying it makes no sense to worry about the affair since Mother is dead and Mr. Shears is gone. Because of Christopher's condition, which leaves him socially and emotionally impaired, this response may in fact reflect his true feelings. But this virtual non-reaction leaves Siobhan, and perhaps the reader, to wonder exactly how Christopher experiences the world.

CHAPTERS 113–137

SUMMARY: CHAPTER 113

Christopher likens his mind to a DVD player that can skip backward through his memories to a specific moment in the past. As an example, he recalls July 4th 1992, when he was nine years old, and describes a family vacation to the beach in Cornwall. His mother sunbathes on a towel, wearing denim shorts and a light blue bikini top. She then goes swimming, even though the water is very cold. Christopher refuses to join her because he doesn't like to swim or take his clothes off. Instead, he rolls up his trousers and walks out into the water. Mother dives out of view and Christopher fears she has been eaten by a shark. As he begins to scream, she reappears. She spreads her fingers into a fan, and when his own spread hand touches hers, he is comforted.

Christopher says that when he meets people he runs a search through his memory to determine if he knows them. He also uses his memory to navigate difficult situations. If someone at school has a seizure, he rewinds his memory to other seizures he has witnessed and then knows what to do. Other people also have pictures in their heads, but unlike Christopher's, their images contain things that are not real or did not happen. His mother was able to imagine an alternate history in which she married a man other than his father.

SUMMARY: CHAPTER 127

When Christopher returns from school, Father is still at work. Christopher goes into the kitchen and puts his things on the table, including his book. He makes a raspberry milkshake and sits down to watch a documentary on underwater life called *Blue Planet*. Father comes home and goes into the kitchen. He returns a few minutes later holding Christopher's book. He speaks quietly and Christopher doesn't realize for a moment that he is angry. Father asks him if the conversation that he had with Mrs. Alexander is true. Christopher replies that it is, and his father grabs him hard, like he never has before. Frightened, Christopher starts to hit his father. After that his memory goes blank. When he comes to, he has blood on his hand and the side of his head hurts. Father's shirt is torn, he has a big scratch on his neck, and he still holds Christopher's book. After a minute, Father goes into the kitchen, and then out into the garden, where Christopher can hear him drop the book into the trash can. When Father comes back into the kitchen, he locks the back door and hides the key to it in a china pot.

SUMMARY: CHAPTER 131
Christopher describes some of the reasons why he hates the colors yellow and brown. Mr. Forbes thinks that hating colors is silly, but Siobhan points out that everyone has favorite colors. Christopher compares his hatred for certain colors to all the arbitrary choices people make in life. If we didn't make choices, he reasons, nothing would ever happen.

SUMMARY: CHAPTER 137
The next day, Father apologizes for hitting him and decides that he will take Christopher to Twycross Zoo to make up for it. At the zoo, Father tells Christopher how much he loves him, and says he was only angry because he doesn't want Christopher to get into trouble by sticking his nose where it doesn't belong. Christopher remembers all the things Father has done for him, like picking him up from the police station, and cooking his meals. To Christopher, love is helping someone when they get into trouble, and telling them the truth. They press their hands together in their substitute for hugging.

ANALYSIS: CHAPTERS 113–137
When Christopher's father discovers Christopher's book, the two have a dramatic confrontation that reveals more detail about Father's character. Though Father never says so explicitly, he appears to have wanted Christopher to drop the investigation so that Christopher wouldn't find out about the affair. This information casts a new light on Father's earlier instruction to Christopher to cease the investigation. Father, we can see, appears not to have worried so much about Christopher digging up other people's business as much as he worried about Christopher digging up the secrets he was keeping himself, suggesting that if this secret comes out it will have serious consequences. The narrative also hints that Christopher's father probably knocked Christopher unconscious during their fight, revealing a violent side to Christopher's father that we've only seen glimpses of to this point. When their altercation turns physical, Christopher appears to black out for a period of time, and when he wakes up he says he has no memory of what happened and that the side of his head hurts, implying he was struck.

In his narration, Christopher doesn't describe himself as having an obvious outward reaction to this fight, but the section of narration that follows the fight hints at a strong emotional response. Immediately after his description of the fight, Christopher goes into a seemingly unrelated commentary on why he hates yellow and brown, and he expresses a sense of disgust toward some of the yellow and brown items he lists, such as feces. Although Christopher doesn't explicitly link these feelings of disgust to his fight with his father, the placement of this section right after the fight implies the link, so even though Christopher doesn't tell the reader outright how he feels, the reader can infer what Christopher feels. In fact, the apparently irrelevant tangents in Christopher's narration often reveal his feelings about the events of the sections just before.

Christopher also describes his memory in great detail in this section, and as he does so he gives the reader more information about Mother. Christopher says that, like a DVD player, he can skip in his mind to a specific time in the past, allowing him to replay the scene in his head exactly as it happened. Many of the memories he recalls to demonstrate the point involve his interactions with Mother. We see them at the beach, for instance, and Mother calming Christopher after he becomes frightened that a shark has attacked her. We also see Mother describing what she imagines her life would have been like had she not married Father. She talks about living in a farmhouse in France with a local handyman named Jean, indicating that she at least fantasized at that point about a different life, and a relationship different from the one she had with Father.

Along with these recollections, Christopher notes that, unlike most people, he remembers things exactly as they happened, which allows him to know whom he has already met and what to do in situations he has already encountered, like when another student at school has a seizure. Christopher implies that, as a counterpart to this ability, he can't imagine a false past, as Mother does when she talks about living in France. But as we have seen through Christopher's dreams of being an astronaut (and through the fantasy he has in the very next chapter as he watches *Blue Planet*, about being in an underwater submersible), he clearly has no difficulty imagining different scenarios in the present and future, indicating that he only has trouble imagining backward in time. Even so, Christopher takes pride in his memory and clearly regards it as one of his strengths.

Chapters 139–151

Summary: Chapter 139

Christopher describes photographs taken in 1917 that appear to show live fairies. The incident was dubbed "The Case of the Cottingley Fairies," and Sir Arthur Conan Doyle, author of the Sherlock Holmes stories, endorsed the photographs as proof of the existence of fairies. In actuality, the fairies shown were just cutouts, which the photographers admitted in 1981. Christopher explains Occam's razor, a law that says "no more things should be presumed to exist than are absolutely necessary." To Christopher, this means that murderers tend to know their victims, fairies don't exist, and you can't talk to the dead.

Summary: Chapter 149

At school, Siobhan asks Christopher why his face is bruised. He explains the fight with Father. Siobhan reluctantly accepts that nothing happened worth worrying over, largely because Christopher cannot remember whether or not Father hit him.

Christopher returns from school before Father gets home from work. Christopher gets the key to the garden from the china pot and sets out to retrieve his book. When he doesn't find his book in the trash can, he realizes Father might have hidden it elsewhere in the house. He eventually discovers the book in a shirt box underneath a toolbox in Father's bedroom closet. Though happy that Father hasn't thrown his book away, he worries that Father will know he has been searching through his things. Just then, Father comes home. Christopher rushes to put everything back the way he found it. At the last moment, he notices a letter in the shirt box addressed to him and sees there are several such letters. He takes one of the letters, puts his book back, and tiptoes back to his room.

Later, Father makes dinner, then begins to set up shelves in the living room. Christopher uses the opportunity to read the letter alone in his room. The letter is from Mother, and it describes a new job she has, working as a secretary in a factory. She tells of the apartment that she has moved into in London with a man named Roger and notes that she has not received any letters back from Christopher. She says she loves him very much anyway. The letter confuses Christopher because Mother never worked at a factory or lived in London. The letter has no date, but on the envelope it bears the postmark "16th of October 1997," eighteen months after

Mother died. Christopher feels excited to have a new mystery on his hands, but he decides not to jump to conclusions. He hides the letter and goes downstairs to watch television.

SUMMARY: CHAPTER 151

Christopher describes scientific mysteries as problems that have yet to be solved. Christopher says ghosts are only a mystery because we do not know the science behind them, but one day we will. He talks about the seemingly random number of frogs in the pond at school from year to year and notes that a formula, discovered by a group of scientists, shows that the population density of frogs runs in predictable cycles that only appear random. Christopher concludes that sometimes complex problems follow simple rules, and that whole populations can die out for no reason other than the way the numbers work.

––––––––––––––––––

ANALYSIS: CHAPTERS 139–151

Christopher's discovery of the letter from Mother adds a dramatic twist to the plot and reveals another secret that Father had kept from Christopher. The letter initially confuses Christopher because it contains facts about Mother's life working at a factory in London, although to Christopher's knowledge Mother had never worked at a factory or lived in London. The postmark dates the letter to several months after Mother's supposed death, leading Christopher, who evidently doesn't consider that Mother might not be dead, to question how this scenario could have occurred. He wonders if perhaps the letter was in the wrong envelope, and he even speculates somewhat comically that it could be a letter to a different Christopher from that Christopher's mother. The reaction creates an irony in which the reader, unlike Christopher, realizes that the letter suggests Mother never died at all, and that Father has likely been lying about this fact as well. Before Christopher considers this possibility, however, he decides not to jump to conclusions without more information, implying that he will soon undertake a new investigation.

Notably, Christopher follows his discovery of the letter from Mother with thoughts on the supernatural and a discussion of Occam's razor, appearing to comment on his own reaction to Mother's letter. Before finding the letter, Christopher talks about "The Case of the Cottingley Fairies," noting with disappointment the variety of people who believed the picture of the fairies to be legitimate. For Christopher, the Cottingley fairies case proves the principle of Occam's razor, which suggests that the simplest explanation tends to be the correct one. When Christopher finds Mother's letter, however, he avoids the simplest explanation—that Mother didn't die as Father said she did. Christopher instead thinks up different reasons a letter from Mother would bear a postmark from after her death, even entertaining the outlandish notion that the letter is actually to another Christopher. He willfully evades the possibility that Mother is alive. Yet talking about the Cottingley fairies and Occam's razor, Christopher remarks that people do not always believe the obvious explanation because they "want to be stupid and they do not want to know the truth." Christopher's digressions into these other subjects draw attention to the discrepancy between his beliefs and his reaction to the letter. Like the people he calls "stupid," Christopher may not want to know the truth, because it may be too uncomfortable to bear. If his mother is alive, it would mean a new set of uncertainties for Christopher to deal with, for instance, where is his mother, why hasn't he heard from her, should he find her? And it would mean that Christopher's father lied to him, suggesting that Christopher doesn't know his father as well as he thinks. Rather than deal with these possibilities, Christopher manufactures other, more complicated explanations. Whether this explanation is accurate or whether Christopher genuinely doesn't make the connection between his mother's letters and her being alive remains unclear, however.

Christopher's talk of ghosts and the seemingly random fluctuations in frog populations also appear to comment on this new mystery regarding Mother, but this discussion emphasizes Christopher's belief that logic and careful thinking can find a rational explanation for any mystery. Christopher, who talks about his uncle's sighting of a ghost in a shopping center, doesn't deny the existence of ghosts, he just believes a scientific explanation for them exists. He compares ghosts to the changes in frog populations, which initially seem random but actually follow a predictable cycle. Similarly, scientists need only to discover the laws that allow ghosts to exist. The fact that Christopher's thoughts on ghosts, supposedly the spiritual remains of dead people, follow just after he finds the letter from Mother, whom he thought was dead, suggests that Christopher sees some link between the two. Similarly, his belief that an explanation for ghosts exists but it just hasn't yet been discovered, implies that Christopher feels an explanation for Mother's letter exists. He just needs to find out what that explanation is.

CHAPTERS 157–163

SUMMARY: CHAPTER 157

On Monday evening, Father goes out to fix a flooded cellar, so Christopher sneaks into Father's room. He counts 43 letters addressed to him in the same handwriting. The first letter describes a memory that Mother has of Christopher playing with a wooden train set she bought him for Christmas. Christopher made time-tables for all of the train lines. Spelling errors occur throughout the letter, like "woodden" and "timetabel." At the bottom it is signed "Love, Your Mum."

In the next letter, Mother explains why she left the family. She recounts a time that Christopher had a fit in a crowded store while she was Christmas shopping. Christopher became frightened by the number of people in the store, and when Mother tried to move him he started screaming and broke two mixers by knocking them off a nearby shelf. Then he wet himself. He wouldn't stop screaming and they had to walk home because Mother knew he wouldn't want to get on a crowded bus. At home, Mother cried to Father, who then became angry with her for being selfish. She describes how she began to feel very lonely and argue with Father a lot. Then she started spending a lot of time with Roger. Roger said he didn't love Eileen (Mrs. Shears) anymore and asked Mother to leave Father for him.

One evening at supper Christopher threw a cutting board, which broke Mother's toes. She had to go to the hospital and couldn't walk for a month. Afterward, Father blamed her for losing her temper. While she recovered, she saw how much more calmly Christopher acted around Father than with her. She decided Christopher and Father would be better off without her in the house and moved in with Roger in London. Father was so angry and hurt by her abandonment that he forbade her from calling Christopher or coming to visit. She ends the letter by asking Christopher to please write her back.

In the next letter, Mother writes about her new job as a secretary in a real estate office. She asks if he received the present she sent. In a fourth letter, Mother talks about going to the dentist with Christopher. Christopher stops reading because he feels sick. He realizes that Mother didn't have a heart attack and that Father has been lying to him. He curls into a ball on the bed and passes out. When he wakes up it is dark outside. He has vomited all over. Father comes into the room, but to Christopher his voice sounds small and distant. Father sees the letters and begins to cry. When Father touches Christopher to guide him to the bath it does not hurt like it usually does.

SUMMARY: CHAPTER 163

Christopher recounts an exercise that Julie, his first teacher at school, had him perform when he was young. In the exercise, Julie showed him a tube of Smarties candy and asked him to guess what was inside. When he guessed Smarties, Julie revealed that the tube contained a little red pencil. Julie then put the pencil back in the tube and asked what Mother or Father would guess were they to come in at that moment. Christopher figured they would say the tube held a little red pencil. Julie told Mother and Father that Christopher would always have difficulty understanding another person's point of view. Christopher no longer has difficulty with these situations, however, because he thinks of them as puzzles to be solved.

Christopher describes an experiment he saw in a TV series called *How the Mind Works*. When a person looks at a page of text, they really only see the small area that their eyes are currently focused on. The mind fills in the image of the rest with an image it presumes to be true. If the text elsewhere on the page changes while the eyes aren't looking at it, the mind doesn't notice. People assume that computers are just machines without minds. But Christopher explains that in actuality the mind is a complicated computer, and that even feelings are just a picture in your mind of what is going to happen tomorrow or next year, or what might have happened instead of what did happen. If it is a happy picture you smile, and if it is a sad picture you cry.

ANALYSIS: CHAPTERS 157–163

Mother's letters, which serve as the only time someone other than Christopher narrates, provide the reader with insight into Mother's character that is uncolored by Christopher's interpretation. Christopher publishes Mother's letters in their entirety, down to spelling errors, and in the letters Mother describes her feelings frankly. For instance, she essentially admits that the stress of caring for Christopher destroyed her marriage with Father and caused her to flee the family. Mother's accounts of Christopher's behavior as a child also allow us to see how much Christopher has progressed in managing his condition, something Christopher has alluded to before. As Mother describes, Christopher's wild tantrums and inability to socialize were far more pronounced when he was younger. Notably, Mother appears to blame herself for some of Christopher's behavior when she observes that Christopher acts more calmly around Father and writes that Christopher and Father might be better off without her. She also openly expresses her guilt at abandoning Christopher, and she assumes when she doesn't hear back from Christopher that Christopher remains too angry with her to write. She evidently doesn't realize Christopher has not received her letters.

Christopher feels deeply hurt by the information that he gains from the letters, as evidenced by the strong physical reaction he has. When he realizes that Mother abandoned him and Father to run away with Mr. Shears (whom she calls by his first name, Roger), and that Father has kept the truth from Christopher for two years, pretending all the while that Mother has died, Christopher passes out and vomits all over himself and his bed. He appears too shocked to feel any sense of relief at knowing that Mother is alive. As we have seen, Christopher measures love in large part by a person's honesty, and he realizes at this point that Father, the person who takes care of him more than anyone, has deceived him. Christopher feels so distraught that for a moment he even forgets his great dislike of being touched and lets Father guide him to the bathtub.

We also gain more insight into the specific details of Christopher's condition in this section. As we see from the exercise he does in chapter 163, in which his teacher reveals that the Smarties tube contains a pencil rather than candy and then makes Christopher guess what another person would think the tube contains, Christopher has trouble recognizing that other people have their own minds. In other words, he has difficulty considering a situation from someone else's point of view. Although Christopher has developed a workaround for this problem, specifically by thinking of these situations as puzzles to be solved, the reader can see that this inability to empathize still affects Christopher's understanding of the world and other people. It plays a particularly large role in Christopher's social impairment and in his inability to recognize the emotions underlying different facial expressions. It keeps Christopher isolated from people in an almost literal sense, in turn making him feel just as comfortable being alone as he feels in the company of other people—or even more comfortable. This deficit is also an important symptom of autism, providing more evidence that Christopher likely has a mild version of the disorder.

CHAPTERS 167–179

SUMMARY: CHAPTER 167

After a bath, Father dries Christopher off and puts him in bed. Father apologizes for lying about Mother and keeping the letters from Christopher. Father doesn't want any more lies between them, so he confesses to killing Wellington. He explains how upset he was when Mother left him. Mrs. Shears helped him to get through it, but when he recently had an argument with Mrs. Shears, she kicked him out of her house, and Wellington attacked him in the yard. Father killed Wellington with the garden fork. Christopher screams in terror at the news, and pushes Father off the bed. Father retreats downstairs, begging Christopher to go to sleep so that they can talk about the situation in the morning. Christopher decides he can't trust Father. Because Father murdered Wellington, Christopher reasons, Father could also murder him. Christopher waits until 1:20 AM, takes out his Swiss Army knife, and walks quietly downstairs. In the living room, Father sleeps on the sofa. Christopher goes into the kitchen, takes his special food box, and steps out into the garden. He hides behind the garden shed and eats two clementines and a Milkybar, then wonders what to do next.

SUMMARY: CHAPTER 173

From the space behind the shed, Christopher can see the constellation Orion. He says people call it Orion because it looks like a hunter with a club, but he says the stars in the constellation can be joined to make any number of shapes, such as a dinosaur. At any rate, he says, Orion is not a hunter: it is a group of 21 stars billions of miles away.

SUMMARY: CHAPTER 179

Christopher sleeps in the garden that night. In the morning, he hides as he hears Father come outside looking for him. After Father leaves, Christopher decides he should live with Mrs. Shears, but when he knocks on her door she doesn't answer. He goes through the reasons he can't live with Siobhan, Uncle Terry, or Mrs. Alexander, then decides to go to London to find Mother. The prospect frightens him because he has never been anywhere on his own before, but the idea of returning to Father's house, or hiding in the garden every night, is far worse.

Christopher notices the circular lid of an old metal pan leaning against the side of Mrs. Shears's house. The pan looks like the surface of a planet, with rust forming continents and islands. The image reminds him of his dream to become an astronaut, and he feels disappointed at how impossible it now seems. Going to London, which is only a hundred miles away, scares him. He would have to travel thousands of miles away as an astronaut.

Christopher goes to Mrs. Alexander's house and tells her he needs someone to watch Toby while he goes to London. He says he is going to live with Mother because Father lied to him about Mother's death and killed Wellington. Mrs. Alexander tries to get him to come inside, but when she says she's going to phone Father, Christopher panics and runs back home. Christopher grabs his schoolbag and fills it with food, a change of clothes, and some math books. He feels afraid when he spots Father's mobile phone and wallet next to the kitchen sink, but remembering that Father's van was not outside, he realizes Father forgot the items. Christopher takes Father's bank card, the pin to which Father told him in case he ever needed it.

Christopher puts Toby in his pocket and walks to school, intending to ask Siobhan the location of the train station. The farther Christopher gets from home the less frightened he feels of Father but the more frightened he feels of being alone. He describes his fear as a mathematical constant.

Christopher sees Father's van in the school parking lot and vomits at the sight. To calm himself, he does cubes of numbers and counts fifty breaths. He decides to ask a stranger for directions to the train station instead. The woman he asks points him in the direction of the station and tells him to follow a bus that is passing. Christopher runs after the bus but can't keep up. He walks on the edge of the road for a while until he spots a railway sign. He starts to walk toward it, but in his confusion he loses sight of the sign. He comes up with a plan. He knows that if something is nearby you can find it by moving in a clockwise spiral, taking every right turn until you come back to a road you have already walked on, then expanding your spiral to streets you haven't checked. In this way, he finds the train station.

ANALYSIS: CHAPTERS 167–179

When Father admits to killing Wellington, the novel finally resolves the initial mystery that set the plot in motion and conclusively ties Wellington's murder to the tangle of relationships Christopher has gradually uncovered between his parents and Mr. and Mrs.

Shears. Over the course of the novel, Christopher's inquiry into Wellington's death has consistently turned up more secret information about Mother and Father than it has about Wellington, turning the investigation of Wellington's murder into a broader symbol of Christopher's search for the truth about his parents. Here, the two investigations finally converge, as Christopher's discovery of Mother's letters also prompts Father to admit to killing Wellington. By this point, the mystery of Wellington's death, which provided the driving force for the early chapters of the novel, has become the less important puzzle, and the history of secret relationships between Mother and Mr. Shears and between Father and Mrs. Shears has taken over.

Christopher's observations on the constellation Orion appear to comment indirectly on the way Christopher now views Father, since Christopher now knows that Father murdered Wellington. Christopher thinks about Orion as he hides outside in the garden, just after Father reveals himself to be Wellington's killer, and both this timing and Christopher's thoughts themselves suggest that Christopher draws a parallel between Father and Orion. Like Orion, which appears to be a hunter but is in truth a series of explosions that exist billions of miles away, Father appears to be one thing, specifically a loving caretaker to Christopher, and in fact turns out to be a liar and a murderer. Christopher's observation that the stars in Orion look as much like any number of things, such as a dinosaur, as they do a hunter also acts as a comment on subjectivity. While one person may see a hunter in the stars that make up Orion, another person—to use an example Christopher gives—could see a teapot. Father, meanwhile, may appear to be a kind man to some, but a person with a different perspective, such as Mrs. Shears or Christopher, can view him quite differently.

The extreme fear Christopher feels toward his father reiterates what the reader has already seen in terms of Christopher's view of social relationships. Christopher feels most comfortable with people when they act predictably. Early in the novel, he says he even feels comfortable being arrested after he hits the officer because arresting someone represents a predictable behavior for a police officer. Christopher's father, on the other hand, has not acted predictably by killing Wellington, and as a result, Father's confession actually frightens Christopher more than it reassures him, even though Father tells Christopher about Wellington because he doesn't want any more lies between them. We've also seen that honesty plays a significant role in Christopher's feelings toward a person, evident from Christopher's description of love. Since Father has lied to Christopher about Mother, then revealed that he acted violently and stabbed Wellington, Christopher doesn't feel safe with Father. He decides to run away, setting in motion the novel's final act.

CHAPTERS 181–199

SUMMARY: CHAPTER 181
Christopher explains that he must memorize every physical detail of his environment. In places he has already visited he can simply note the changes that have occurred since his last time there. But if Christopher is in an entirely new place, processing his surroundings can cause his mind to freeze up, like a computer crash. Most people are not like this, and only glance at their surroundings before moving on. In a field in the countryside they might notice some cows. In the same field, Christopher would memorize the exact number of cows, their colors, and their placement. Christopher attributes the fact that he is good at math and logic to his attention to detail.

SUMMARY: CHAPTER 191
Christopher waits in the entrance of the station, feeling sick from the crowded, smelly underpass tunnel before him. He goes through the tunnel and his head starts to hurt from the numerous signs offering goods and services. He sits down outside a café and does a problem called "Conway's Soldiers" in his head to calm himself. The puzzle involves jumping colored tiles over each other on a chessboard that stretches infinitely in all directions.

A policeman interrupts Christopher, asking why he has been sitting in the café in a trance for two and a half hours. Christopher says he is going to visit his mother in London. The policeman asks if he has a ticket, or money for a ticket. Christopher explains that he has neither but that his father gave him his ATM card to pay for the trip. The policeman escorts him to a cash machine, where Christopher withdraws fifty pounds. After the policeman points him to the ticket window, Christopher purchases a one-way ticket to London. To get to the train platform he has to go through the underpass again. This time he imagines a big red line stretching across the floor to his destination. He follows the line by putting one foot in front of the other while saying out loud "left, right, left, right." He pretends that the people he bumps into along the way are Guarding Demons in an imagined computer game called "Train to London" and pushes past them. He finally reaches the train, and he boards it.

SUMMARY: CHAPTER 193

Christopher used to make timetables for all his toy trains and for himself. Christopher explains that time is not like space. If you put down an object you can draw a map back to it, or remember its location. The object physically exists in space where you left it. But time is the relationship between events and is not a fixed relationship. If you travel near the speed of light in a spaceship you may come back to find that everyone you know is dead, while you remain young. If you get lost in a desert you are in a desert, but if you get lost in time you are nowhere at all. Christopher likes timetables because they make sure that he does not get lost in time.

SUMMARY: CHAPTER 197

The claustrophobia he feels in the packed train reminds Christopher of when the school bus broke down, leaving Mother to drive Christopher and some other children home. The car was so full that Christopher jumped out while it was moving, hurting his head. The policeman from earlier appears. He says Father is looking for Christopher and that he has come to take Christopher back to the station. But the train starts to move, so the policeman has to wait until the next stop.

As they travel, Christopher looks out the train window. He begins to feel dizzy as he realizes the millions of miles of train track that must exist in the world, and the millions of people that must have laid them. Christopher, not knowing the train has a restroom, wets his pants. The policeman orders Christopher to go clean up, and when Christopher enters the restroom there is poop smeared on the toilet seat. The sight sickens him. When he is done, he notices that across from the restroom are two shelves that remind Christopher of the cupboard back home where he often went to feel safe. He climbs into the middle shelf and pulls a suitcase in front of him. He does some quadratic equations to pass the time. The train begins to slow down and he hears the policeman knocking on the door of the restroom, then leaving. Christopher stays perfectly still until the train starts moving again.

SUMMARY: CHAPTER 199

Christopher thinks that people believe in God illogically, because they do not realize that unlikely things can happen by chance. He illustrates the three conditions needed to result in life: Replication, Mutation, and Heritability. He says humans are animals just like any other, only luckier evolutionarily. One day an animal will evolve that will be smarter than humans are, or humans will catch a disease and die out, leaving some other creature to be the best animal.

ANALYSIS: CHAPTERS 181–199

In this section, the majority of which watches Christopher navigating the train station as he tries to get to London, we see more of the difficulties Christopher has with everyday activities as a result of his condition. In a scene illustrating perhaps the greatest disadvantage of his condition, Christopher quickly feels overwhelmed as he moves through the station, to the point that he can barely function. He prefaces his journey by explaining in chapter 181 the trouble that his mind has processing new surroundings. His extreme attention to detail—the quality that allows him to excel in math and science—helps him to create a photographic memory of a location, but it can also become a liability when he finds himself in a situation where he has to take in a huge amount of information in very little time. The train station, with its large crowds and multitude of signs and shops, overloads him with information, essentially causing him to shut down. In addition, for the first time in his life Christopher finds himself alone and without any caretaker to rely on. Without an adult or his daily routine, Christopher feels lost, both in terms of his location and in time, as he describes it, evident in that he ends up sitting outside a café for two and a half hours doing little more than staring.

Simultaneously, however, we see how resilient Christopher can be when necessary and how much progress he has made in dealing with the limitations of his condition when he recalls episodes from when he was younger. Notably, even though Christopher shuts down at times, we also see him repeatedly finding ways to cope with the difficult situations he encounters. For instance, Christopher imagines himself to be in a video game, allowing him to pay attention specifically to solving the problems he encounters as if they were puzzles. To get to the train, Christopher also envisions a red line traversing the floor, and then focuses on following that line, to the exclusion of everything else around him. These coping strategies represent a great deal of progress for Christopher. In contrast, he describes a time when he was younger and the bus to school broke down, so Mother had to take Christopher and others to school.

Christopher became so panicked that he literally jumped out of a moving car, hurting himself as a result. While Christopher clearly still has difficulties just getting through a loud and crowded environment as a result of his condition, he nonetheless has made great strides in learning to compensate for his limitations.

In his digressions, Christopher reveals more about his view of the world when he offhandedly dismisses the importance of beauty and belief in God, both of which he seems to think of as illogical. When Christopher discusses the way he processes a new environment, he contrasts his approach with that of the average person. He condescendingly calls what the average person does "glancing," essentially meaning the person notices a few details about the scene, that some cows stand in a field for instance, and that's all. They stop noticing details, Christopher says, because they think about other things, such as the beauty of the place. Christopher's tone indicates that he places little value on beauty, particularly compared to hard facts like the number of cows and what colors they are. Beauty apparently doesn't affect him emotionally, and it can't be measured or mapped in a way that he understands. He sees it as illogical and unnecessary, so he disregards it. Similarly, Christopher thinks of God as an illogical and unnecessary idea. He speaks disdainfully of people who believe in God, suggesting they do so only because they need a simple explanation for complicated matters such as the existence of life on Earth and the presence of complex features like eyes in living things. Christopher believes you can explain life and complex features without bringing God into the discussion; therefore no reason exists to believe in God (Christopher's reasoning here recalls the concept of Occam's razor, which says one shouldn't presume a thing to exist unless it is necessary). In Christopher's understanding of the world, both beauty and God are superfluous, so he dismisses them.

CHAPTERS 211–229

SUMMARY: CHAPTER 211

The train continues traveling, and Christopher attempts to judge the distance he has gone by noting the amount of time between stops. When the train stops again, Christopher leaves his hiding place. He sees a policeman in the next car and gets off the train. The station he enters overwhelms him again. He imagines his red line and follows it to the far end of the station. A man tells him a policeman is looking for him, but Christopher keeps on walking. The huge number of signs makes all of them incomprehensible to Christopher. He makes his hands into a tube and looks through it in order to focus on one sign at a time. He follows the sign that reads "Information" to a small shop and asks if he is in London. The shopkeeper says he is. When he asks the way to Mother's address she tells him to take the subway to Willesden Junction or Willesden Green, and points him in the right direction.

In the subway, he hides in a photo booth. Through its curtain he watches people purchase tickets and enter the subway station. He gets up the courage to go and buy his own ticket from a machine, then follows the signs to his platform. People begin to fill the station and Christopher starts to feel very sick. Trains keep pulling in and leaving, but Christopher can only sit paralyzed on the bench, wishing he were at home but unable to go there, because Father murdered Wellington.

SUMMARY: CHAPTER 223

Christopher describes an advertisement for Malaysia located opposite him on the platform while he remains frozen in the station. Christopher doesn't see the point of going on holiday to see new things and relax when a person can always discover new things where he is. Christopher gives the example of filling glasses with different amounts of water to form different musical notes when you run your finger along the rim.

SUMMARY: CHAPTER 227

Christopher sits in a trance for five hours on the platform before realizing that Toby has run away. Christopher spots Toby between the tracks among some other mice and climbs onto the tracks to get him. The sound of an approaching train grows louder, and a man runs forward to haul Christopher, clutching Toby, back onto the platform. The man shouts at Christopher for being so reckless, and a woman approaches to ask if there is anything she can do to help. Christopher tells her to back away, revealing that he has his Swiss Army knife. The man and woman both leave Christopher alone and get on the next train.

After eight more trains pass by, Christopher decides to board. He stays on the train until Willesden Junction, where he gets off. He approaches a shop and asks for directions. The shopkeeper sells him a book called *London AZ Street Atlas and Index* for £2.95. He uses the atlas to get to Mother's address, but no one answers when

Christopher rings the bell. He sits down to wait. At 11:32 PM he hears Mother's voice as she approaches the apartment. Mother tries to hug Christopher but he pushes her away. She spreads her fingers out into a fan instead, and they touch hands. Mr. Shears is with Mother. Christopher tells her about his frightening journey from Swindon.

Inside the flat Mother draws Christopher a bath. She sits down next to the bath and asks why Christopher never wrote to her. Christopher explains that Father kept all the letters hidden in his closet and said Mother was dead. A policeman comes to the door of the apartment and says Father reported Christopher as a runaway. The policeman asks Christopher if he wants to go back to Father or if he prefers to stay with Mother. Christopher chooses to stay with Mother, and the policeman leaves. Exhausted, Christopher goes to bed on an air mattress in the spare room. He wakes up to the sound of Father shouting in the living room at 2:31 AM. Mother, Mr. Shears, and Father have a heated argument. Father bursts through the door of the spare room to find Christopher, who has his Swiss Army knife open and ready. Father cries and apologizes and spreads his fingers out in a fan, but Christopher refuses to touch him. The policeman comes back and escorts Father from the flat. Christopher goes back to sleep.

SUMMARY: CHAPTER 229

That night, Christopher dreams that a virus has killed nearly everyone on Earth. A person can catch the virus just by looking at someone who has it, even if the infected person is on television. The virus spreads very quickly until the only people left on Earth are people like Christopher who do not look at other people's faces. In the dream, he can go anywhere he likes without fear of someone touching him or asking him questions. He can drive and if he bumps into things, it doesn't matter. At the end of the dream he goes home to Father's house in Swindon, only Father is gone. He makes himself Gobi Aloo Sag with red food coloring, watches a video about the solar system, plays computer games, and goes to bed. When he awakens from the dream, he feels happy.

ANALYSIS: CHAPTERS 211–229

Christopher's successful arrival in London marks perhaps his greatest accomplishment in the novel and a significant step in his journey toward independence. Since Christopher has never traveled alone before this trip, taking the train by himself all the way to London presents a daunting task. In several ways, the trip epitomizes everything Christopher finds uncomfortable about the world. He has to navigate through large crowds where he is touched frequently, he has to navigate an unfamiliar environment, and he has to process large amounts of new information, which actually overwhelms him to the point that he shuts down at times. By meeting these challenges, Christopher proves to himself that he can overcome any obstacle on his own. In other words, he doesn't need his father to take care of him and can live independently.

Christopher's journey to London takes on the qualities of an adventure story. While the experience of walking through a subway station and getting on the right train would be ordinary for many people, for Christopher these tasks present a significant challenge, mainly due to his condition and his inexperience with such situations. The large crowds and the huge influx of information Christopher experiences become life threatening in his mind, and he even says he can't remember the exact details of the ad for Malaysia he saw in the station because he thought he "was going to die." The novel communicates this experience to the reader with a series of hurried, breathless sentences that reflect Christopher's distress and confusion, such as "And there was sweat running down my face from under my hair and I was moaning, not groaning, but different, like a dog when it has hurt its paw, and I heard the sound but I didn't realize it was me at first." The section even includes a situation that could have been genuinely fatal in which Christopher climbs onto the train tracks to retrieve Toby and narrowly avoids being hit by a train.

Chapter 227, which marks the climax of the novel, effectively brings the major action of the story to a close while establishing one additional conflict to be settled: Christopher, Mother, and Father must come to terms with one another. When Christopher's father comes to find him in London, after Christopher has reunited with his mother, we see for the first time Christopher, Mother, and Father interacting face-to-face. By this point, the relationships between the three characters have changed significantly, putting the situation at the beginning of the novel—Christopher living with his father and his mother absent from their lives—in flux. Christopher now knows his mother is alive and he intends to live with her in London. He also fears his father to the point that he's afraid to be in the same room with him. Christopher's mother, meanwhile, wants to be part of Christopher's life again, while Christopher's father is in danger of losing his place in Christopher's life (the only relationship that hasn't changed is the relationship between Christopher's mother and father, who continue to dislike each other). As a result, Christopher's life has become disordered. Christopher, Mother, and Father will have to work through their issues with one another to reestablish an ordered, stable life for Christopher, creating a final conflict to solve.

In chapter 229, Christopher again dreams of being almost entirely alone on Earth, giving him a sense of relief after his dramatic trip to London while also reflecting his desire to be independent. In contrast with his experience in the overcrowded underpass tunnel, Christopher's dream makes him one of the few survivors on the planet after a virus wipes out most of the population. This scenario represents an ideal life to Christopher. He could live without having to interact with other people and without worrying about other nuisances like someone touching him, which the reader has seen repeatedly to be something Christopher finds distressing. Perhaps more importantly, Christopher would be able to make his own decisions (an ordinary desire for a teenager). He says he wouldn't have to go anywhere he didn't want to go, he could eat anything he wanted, and he could play computer games for an entire week if he chose. Notably, he says Father's house would now be his, because Father would be dead. Christopher expresses no sadness or remorse at this thought, but rather appears to enjoy the idea of living without his father, who has been the primary authority figure in Christopher's life. Significantly, in the dream Christopher doesn't replace his father with anyone, such as his mother or Siobhan, but imagines living on his own and taking care of himself. The fantasy suggests that Christopher has a growing desire for independence not just from his father, but from authority figures generally.

CHAPTER 233

SUMMARY

Christopher awakens in Mother's apartment. While he eats breakfast, Mr. Shears and Mother argue over how long Christopher can stay. Mother takes a leave from work to care for Christopher. She takes him shopping for items he needs, such as pajamas, but she has to take Christopher home when he becomes frightened in a store. Christopher tells Mother he must return to Swindon to take his

A-level math test, but Mother says she doesn't know if that will be possible. That night, Christopher can't sleep, so around 2 AM he goes out into the street and takes a walk. Mother comes out of the apartment shouting his name, scared that he has run away. She finds him and makes him promise never to leave the apartment on his own again.

A few days later, Mother is fired from her job for taking leave. Christopher demands to be taken to Swindon to take his A-level test. Mother insists the test can be postponed. The next morning, Christopher tries to forecast the day by looking out the dining room window. He sees five red cars in a row followed by four yellow cars in a row, invalidating his system. Mother takes him to watch the planes take off and land from Heathrow airport. She says she has phoned Mrs. Gascoyne to postpone his A-level test until next year. Christopher screams at the news.

Every night Mother and Mr. Shears argue. Christopher takes the little radio from the kitchen and leaves the tuner between stations so that the white noise drowns out their arguing and keeps him from thinking about the A-level test. One night Mr. Shears comes into the spare room and wakes Christopher up. Christopher can tell that Mr. Shears has been drinking. Mr. Shears accuses him of not caring about the people around him. Mother pulls Mr. Shears out of the room before he can say anything more.

The next morning, Mother and Christopher leave for Swindon, taking Mr. Shears's car. Mother explains that if they stayed in London any longer someone would get hurt. In Swindon, they go to Father's house. Christopher plays Minesweeper in his room. He hears Father arrive home from work, so he pushes his bed up against his bedroom door to prevent Father from entering. Mother and Father argue in the living room. Father leaves to stay with Rhodri for a few weeks. Christopher again begs to take his A-level test, but Mother has already postponed it. Christopher compares the feeling he gets at hearing this to holding your thumb against a hot radiator. That night, he does not eat and has trouble sleeping.

The next day, Mother takes Christopher to school. Siobhan tells Christopher that Mrs. Gayscone still has his A-level test sealed on her desk, and that they are going to try to get Reverend Peters to come over so Christopher can take his test after all. Christopher feels excited but also tired from not sleeping the night before. That afternoon, Christopher begins his first section of the exam. He reads through it and has trouble thinking of the answers. He feels so frustrated that he wants to stab someone with his Swiss Army knife, but he counts prime numbers in his head to relax. Then he rushes to complete the test. That night, Father comes to the house again, so Christopher hides in the garden until Father leaves.

The next day, Christopher takes part two of the exam. That evening, Mr. Shears throws a large box of Mother's belongings on the lawn, then gets in his car and drives away.

Christopher finishes the exam the following day. Father comes to the house that night and asks Christopher how the exam went. Christopher doesn't answer until Mother encourages him to. The following week, Father asks Mother to move out. She gets a job at a garden center and a doctor prescribes medication for her depression. She and Christopher move into a room in a brick house that Christopher doesn't like for many reasons, primarily that the bed is in the kitchen and that they share the bathroom with strangers. He has to stay at Father's house after school each day because Mother doesn't get off work until 5:30 PM Christopher locks himself in his room so that Father can't get in, and sometimes Father talks to him through the door but Christopher doesn't answer. Toby dies of old age at two years and seven months. Christopher buries him in the soil in a plastic plant pot because Mother's house doesn't have a garden.

One day after school Father sits Christopher down. Father says Christopher's trust is more important to him than anything else. To start rebuilding that trust, Father gives Christopher a two-month-old Golden Retriever. Christopher names her Sandy. The puppy has to stay at Father's house because there isn't enough space in the one-room apartment Christopher shares with Mother, but Christopher can visit whenever he wants. The next week, Christopher learns he got an A on his A-level math test. He spends some nights in Father's house and feels okay with Sandy sleeping on the bed. He plants a vegetable patch in the garden with Father. He buys a book to help him study for his next set of A-level tests.

Christopher sets out a series of goals for the future: to get A grades in A-level Further Math and A-level Physics, so that he can attend college in another town, where he will live in an apartment with a garden and a proper bathroom with Sandy, his books, and his computer. He will graduate with a first-class honors degree and become a scientist. He knows that he can do all of these things because he went to London on his own, solved the mystery of who killed Wellington, found his mother, and wrote a book. And that means he can do anything.

ANALYSIS

Transition is a prominent theme in the book's final chapter, and much of the chapter involves the characters adapting to new situations. Christopher, for instance, lives with his mother now and has to adjust to living in a new place without his father. He also loses his pet rat Toby, who dies of old age. Christopher's mother and father, meanwhile, face their own challenges as they deal with the new way Christopher figures into each of their lives. Mother in particular has a hard time adjusting to having Christopher in her life again because of Christopher's difficult behavior, as seen when he becomes frightened in the store and she has to take him home. The book suggests, however, that these hardships will lead to happiness for the characters. Christopher gets a new puppy to compensate for Toby's death, for instance, and his mother begins to settle down with a new job, a new apartment, and begins to get help for her depression. Christopher and his father also plant a vegetable patch, which serves as a metaphor for how their relationship will eventually grow, suggesting even the rift between them will be repaired.

In the challenges Christopher's mother faces with this transitional phase, the reader also sees the effect that Christopher's condition has on her, giving the reader more insight into why she left Christopher and his father years before. Mother frequently feels frustrated by Christopher's behavior and by his inability to sympathize with her or understand her position on an emotional level. She finds Christopher indifferent to her needs, for instance, when she tries to explain to him that she cannot take him to Swindon for his A-level math test. In taking care of Christopher, she additionally loses her job and frequently argues with Mr. Shears and Christopher's father (the reader doesn't see the arguments with Father for the most part, but Mother tells Christopher that he is threatening to take her to court). She appears overwhelmed by the stress, and we learn that she also suffers from depression, a detail Christopher mentions in passing when he says the doctor gave her pills to keep her from feeling sad. These details help clarify Mother's decision to leave years earlier by showing how emotionally taxing she finds caring for Christopher, and as the novel concludes we see the sacrifices she makes to become part of his life again.

As the novel ends, Christopher talks about his goals for the future, demonstrating a greater confidence in himself and his ability to be independent that stems from his accomplishments over the course of the novel. Notably, Christopher's plans for his future include living on his own. Although he doesn't say so explicitly, the fact that he lists living in an apartment by himself alongside goals like becoming a scientist suggests that being independent would represent a significant triumph to Christopher. It also implies that he recognizes the ways in which his condition limits him. Christopher, however, says he knows he can accomplish these goals because of his recent achievements, specifically going to London by himself, solving the mystery of Wellington's murder, acting bravely when he felt afraid, and writing his book. In other words, he has proven to himself that he can live—and thrive—on his own.

Despite the chapter's suggestion that things will improve for Christopher and his parents, the chapter also reiterates the notion that disorder exists as an inherent part of life. Although Christopher and Father have made significant progress in restoring their bond, they still remain distant from one another when compared with how close they were at the start of the book. Moreover, Christopher no longer lives with Father, and he still distrusts Father to a large degree. Instead, he lives with his mother in a small, unpleasant apartment as Mother struggles, often with great difficulty, to reorder her life. His relationships with both parents remain fragmented since he doesn't trust Father and hasn't spent any significant amount of time with Mother in years. His parents also haven't fully reconciled with one another by the novel's close, yet each wants to be present in Christopher's life. Consequently, Christopher exists in an uneasy triangle with his mother and father. He appears joyful regardless, implying that disorder, while challenging at times, particularly for a character like Christopher who needs order and routine, doesn't prevent happiness if one can learn to live with it.

Important Quotations Explained

1. "This is a murder mystery novel."

Christopher, who opens chapter 7 with this quote just after finding Wellington's dead body, uses some basic conventions of murder mystery stories, but he also diverges from convention frequently, and both approaches give us insight into his character. Christopher chooses to write his book as a murder mystery because he likes the genre, and his taste for murder mysteries stems from a fascination with Sir Arthur Conan Doyle's stories about Sherlock Holmes. These stories, in particular *The Hound of the Baskervilles*, provide Christopher with a template for his own story's structure. Like many of these stories, Christopher's story opens with a murder, then follows Christopher as he investigates the murder and uncovers a larger conspiracy—that conspiracy being the secrets he learns about his parents. Using this framework gives Christopher a way to organize his story, giving him a sense of order and control over his story, and by extension the events of his life, in the same way that timetables give him a sense of order and control over his time.

Moreover, Christopher admires and identifies with the character of Sherlock Holmes, and though he never openly acknowledges this motivation, telling his story as a murder mystery allows him to cast himself in the role of Holmes. The traits Holmes uses to solve his mysteries, such as his strong observational skills, the ability to focus his attention entirely on one problem, and his talent for solving puzzles, Christopher sees as his own strongest traits. Christopher, who recognizes that his condition leaves him with distinct weaknesses, notably his inability to imagine what other people are thinking, looks for ways to emphasize his strengths, and telling his story as a murder mystery allows him to assume the role of Holmes, providing him with a way to play up his strengths and downplay his weaknesses. This mindset, in addition to his solving Wellington's murder and traveling to London by himself, helps Christopher to discover the self-confidence and new sense of independence we see in him at the end of the novel.

Christopher's story ceases to follow the murder-mystery template, most notably when he interjects his commentary on subjects, like math and physics, that seemingly don't relate to the plot. These interjections often tell the reader about Christopher's emotional state, even when he doesn't talk about his feelings explicitly. For example, when Christopher hides out in the garden behind the house after his father admits to killing Wellington, Christopher seems to comment indirectly on his feelings toward his father by talking about the constellation Orion. Christopher implies that his father, who appears to be a loving caretaker but is actually a murderer and liar, is like Orion; it seems to be the outline of a hunter but in reality is just a group of stars billions of miles away. These digressions from the murder-mystery formula regularly follow chapters in which Christopher encounters a dramatic situation.

2.   "I think I would make a very good astronaut. To be a good astronaut you have to be intelligent and I'm intelligent. You also have to understand how machines work and I'm good at understanding how machines work. You also have to be someone who would like being on their own in a tiny spacecraft thousands and thousands of miles away…"

This quote occurs at the beginning of chapter 83, which takes place just after Christopher tells his father that Mr. Shears is his prime suspect in Wellington's murder and Father angrily orders Christopher to drop the investigation. Christopher's dream of being an astronaut represents a fantasy of escape from his current situation, living under his father's authority. The quote comes just after his father reprimands him for not obeying, suggesting that Christopher at this moment greatly feels the need to break away from his father and be on his own. At this point in the story, he has already begun rebelling against his father, lying to him by promising he will drop the investigation but continuing it anyway, for instance. He has also started planning to go away to college, where he imagines he will live on his own. Both activities point to Christopher's growing desire for independence, being an astronaut representing the farthest extreme of this independence, as Christopher would literally be thousands of miles from Earth and his father's authority.

Christopher's wish to be an astronaut is also closely linked to his condition, specifically the difficulty he has with social situations. Christopher, who recognizes that his condition makes him different—and in some people's opinions, less capable—than the average boy his age, repeatedly emphasizes that he is no less able than anyone else, and throughout the novel we see him seeking a role where he feels comfortable and valued. He dislikes his school, for instance, because he feels out of place, as he thinks he's superior to his classmates and being in school with them implies he is somehow less valuable as a person. Becoming an astronaut would prove his worth by allowing him to put to use not only his intelligence and mathematical abilities, but also by turning his poor social skills, which cause him to prefer being alone, into an asset. In that scenario, his condition would make him more valuable, not less.

3.   "Mr. Jeavons said that I liked maths because it was safe. He said I liked maths because it meant solving problems, and these problems were difficult and interesting but there was always a straightforward answer at the end. And what he meant was that maths wasn't like life because in life there are no straightforward answers at the end."

Having just learned of his mother's affair with Mr. Shears, Christopher begins chapter 101 with this quote. With this new information about his mother, Christopher, who initially regarded investigating Wellington's murder as something like a math problem to be solved, has quickly become caught in a much more complicated and uncomfortable situation. By placing Mr. Jeavons's observation just after his discovery of his mother's secret affair, Christopher implies a contrast between math, which is "safe" and yields straightforward answers even to complex problems, and the much more complex affairs of his life. Through this contrast, Christopher suggests that his situation has no clear solution and makes him feel insecure and unsafe. The situation represents the exact opposite of math, a subject Christopher enjoys and feels confident with, in that it leaves him uncertain how to handle the news of his mother's affair, or in other words, how to "solve" the problem.

The quote, however, applies beyond just Christopher's discovery of his mother's infidelity. Christopher finds many aspects of his life confusing and unclear, particularly the social interactions he must deal with every day. He takes refuge in math and subjects such as physics and astronomy because they have clear rules, making them easier to understand, and he enjoys their puzzlelike qualities (Christopher also notes earlier in the book that a good murder mystery is like a puzzle). In fact, in his narration he often embarks on one of his tangents about math or science after dealing with a particularly stressful situation, suggesting that he uses these digressions at times to comfort himself. For instance, after Christopher finds Wellington dead and the police officer arrests Christopher for hitting him, Christopher digresses into a discussion of why the Milky Way looks the way it does. These subjects, governed by logic and laws, possess the predictability and order that Christopher would like, but doesn't have, in his own life.

4.   "And this shows that sometimes people want to be stupid and they do not want to know the truth.
      And it shows that something called Occam's razor is true. And Occam's razor is not a razor that men shave with but a Law, and it says . . .
      No more things should be presumed to exist than are absolutely necessary."

This quote appears toward the end of chapter 139 in Christopher's discussion of the Cottingley fairies hoax, just before Christopher finds his mother's letters in Father's closet. Christopher places great value on logic and reason, and he criticizes the various people who believed the Cottingley fairies hoax for what he sees as their irrational and illogical approach to the incident. He thinks they were not able to see through the hoax simply because they didn't want to, meaning they preferred to believe the lie—that fairies exist—rather than the truth, that fairies aren't real. Christopher sees the incident as validation of the concept called Occam's razor, which basically sums up his approach to anything supernatural or without an obvious explanation, including ghosts and God. Christopher doesn't believe in these things because they are, in his opinion, irrational and unnecessary to explain the world, a job he thinks best left to science.

When Christopher finds his mother's letters in the next chapter, however, he makes exactly the same logical error he criticizes here, apparently ignoring the obvious explanation in favor of the one he prefers to believe. Recognizing that the letters bear a postmark from eighteen months after the date of his mother's supposed death, Christopher comes up with various reasons for this discrepancy, including the possibility that the letter was to another Christopher from that Christopher's mother. He doesn't think of the letters as evidence that his mother did not die. The parallel between the quote and his reaction to the discovery of his mother's letters implies that Christopher, like the people he criticizes, doesn't want to know the truth. He may find it too painful to handle since it would mean that his father has been lying to him and that he now has to deal with the very complicated emotions involved in figuring out what to do about his mother.

5.   "And when I was asleep I had one of my favorite dreams . . .
       And in the dream nearly everyone on the earth is dead . . ."

In chapter 229, having made the difficult trip to London and found his mother, Christopher has what he calls one of his "favorite" dreams. Since the dream is Christopher's fantasy, the fact that he identifies this dream as a favorite implies that it fulfills some of his deepest wishes. First, without anyone else around, Christopher would not have to have any social interactions, which he finds confusing and uncomfortable. He would also not have to deal with crowds, which frighten him, and no one would touch him, which he also greatly dislikes. Significantly, the only people left alive in the dream are people who Christopher says are like him, meaning people with the same condition. If only people with the same condition remained alive, Christopher would be a typical person, rather than an atypical person as he currently is, revealing Christopher's strong desire to no longer feel like an outsider.

Moreover, Christopher likes this dream because if everyone on Earth were dead, he would no longer have any authority figures telling him how to live. Throughout the novel, Christopher has rebelled against his father's authority and displayed a growing desire for independence, culminating in his journey alone to London. Notably, Christopher does not feel sad his father is dead in the dream—he even appears to enjoy living without his father—and no other authority figure, such as his mother, replaces his father, meaning Christopher must take care of himself. These details reveal Christopher's developing sense of maturity, and they lead us to infer that the dream is a favorite because it also fulfills Christopher's wish to live as an adult, making his own decisions and caring for himself.

QUOTATIONS

KEY FACTS

FULL TITLE
The Curious Incident of the Dog in the Night-Time

AUTHOR
Mark Haddon

TYPE OF WORK
Novel

GENRE
Mystery novel; family drama; children's book

LANGUAGE
English

TIME AND PLACE WRITTEN
Early 2000s, Oxford, England

DATE OF FIRST PUBLICATION
2003

PUBLISHER
Vintage Contemporaries, a division of Random House Publishing Inc.

NARRATOR
The novel's mildly autistic protagonist, Christopher John Francis Boone, narrates in the first person.

POINT OF VIEW
Christopher John Francis Boone speaks in the first person. We are to understand the book as his written account of the murder of his neighbor's dog, Wellington. Structurally, the novel alternates between a chapter advancing the narrative, and a chapter in which Christopher discusses ideas or concepts important to him.

TONE
Conversational and matter-of-fact.

TENSE
Past tense

SETTING (TIME)
1998

SETTING (PLACE)
In and around Swindon, England, with a trip to London.

PROTAGONIST
Christopher John Francis Boone

MAJOR CONFLICT
Christopher's investigation of Wellington's murder leads him to uncover a number of secrets about his parents, causing him to lose his trust in Father and to set out to London in search of Mother.

RISING ACTION
As Christopher investigates Wellington's murder, he learns that Mother and Mr. Shears had an affair, that Father and Mrs. Shears also had an affair, that Mother is alive and Father has been lying about her death, and that Father killed Wellington because he was angry with Mrs. Shears.

CLIMAX
After a harrowing journey on his own to London in which he must overcome the limits of his condition, Christopher reunites with his mother.

FALLING ACTION
Christopher moves in with Mother, successfully completes his A-level test in math, and begins to reestablish trust with Father. He recalls all he has accomplished over the course of the novel and sets out a series of goals for the future.

THEMES
The Struggle to Become Independent; Subjectivity; the Disorder of Life; Coping with Loss

MOTIFS
Frustration with Christopher; Science and Technology; Animals

SYMBOLS
The Murder Investigation; Logic Puzzles, Math Problems, and Maps; The A-Level Test in Math

KEY FACTS

FORESHADOWING

Father's excessive anger over Christopher's desire to investigate Wellington's murder; Christopher's repeated observation that murderers typically know their victims; Christopher's discovery of a letter from Mother in Father's closet.

STUDY QUESTIONS & ESSAY TOPICS

STUDY QUESTIONS

1. *Christopher employs a number pictographs— drawings, maps, and figures—over the course of his narrative. Identify a key pictograph in the novel, describe how Christopher uses it, and explain what insight it grants into his character.*

Christopher's drawing of the constellation Orion serves as the pictograph that's most telling of Christopher's character. Christopher uses his drawing to illustrate the manner in which constellations are formed by connecting the stars with imaginary lines. He argues, however, that constellations do not form one shape more than any other. An observer can connect the stars however he chooses to create practically any shape he wants. He changes the lines that make up Orion to show a dinosaur instead as a means of illustrating his point. In a similar way, Christopher believes that his condition is only a handicap from a certain perspective. As an example, he compares his "special needs" to Siobhan's poor eyesight, which requires her to wear glasses. While Christopher recognizes that his condition limits him socially, he also knows he has exceptional abilities in subjects like math and science and feels he is no more handicapped than Siobhan is. In addition, Christopher's thoughts on constellations reflect his emphasis on logical and scientific thinking, which in turn leads him to view many of humanity's popularly held beliefs—such as the existence of heaven—as convenient fantasies with no basis in reality. Just as people look at the stars and imagine the shape of a hunter, Christopher believes people similarly manufacture fantasies about subjects they find frightening or complicated, such as what happens when a person dies. In an earlier chapter when Christopher talks about Mother's death, he says she didn't go to heaven because heaven doesn't exist. Instead, her body has degraded into the soil and been taken up as nutrients by plants. Here, he says the stars don't actually form any shape at all, and in fact they are really nuclear explosions billions of miles away.

2.   *Christopher's condition causes him to see the world in a very subjective way, and as a result the reader may often interpret events differently from Christopher. What role does this difference between Christopher's understanding of events and the reader's understanding of events play in the novel?*

Christopher lacks the ability to fully understand what takes place in the minds of other people, as shown early in the novel by his inability to identify a person's mood from their facial expression. As a result, at many times in the novel Christopher fails to understand another character's intentions. The reader, on the other hand, may recognize Christopher's misunderstanding, resulting in a gap between Christopher's view of events and the reader's view. For instance, although Christopher becomes afraid of Father when he begins to think Father capable of murdering him, the reader can see that this reaction is excessive. This gap lends the novel a sense of irony throughout and makes the novel comic at times, as when we see characters become frustrated at their inability to make Christopher understand them. But this ironic gap also emphasizes the idea that each person has a unique view of the world. A great deal of the novel, including many of Christopher's digressions, helps the reader to understand the world as Christopher sees it. While we sometimes see Christopher as ridiculous, as when he leaves the house of his elderly neighbor, Mrs. Alexander, when she goes inside to get him cookies, we also come to sympathize with Christopher in his struggles. We see, for instance, how he suffers when he realizes that Mother did not die and Father has been lying to him. The novel becomes alternately funny and moving as a result, thereby creating much of its emotional impact on the reader.

3.   *To what extent is Christopher's condition responsible for the conflicts that arise in* THE CURIOUS INCIDENT OF THE DOG IN THE NIGHT-TIME?

Christopher's condition directly results in a few minor conflicts in the novel, but more significantly, it factors to different degrees in the major conflicts between Mother and Father, between Father and Mrs. Shears, and between Father and Christopher. The minor conflicts often arise from Christopher's trouble with social interaction. Early in the novel, for instance, Christopher hits the policeman because Christopher severely dislikes being touched. The policeman arrests Christopher, so Father has to come pick him up, leading to a small argument between Father and Christopher as they drive home from the police station.

The larger conflicts, however, tend to result indirectly from the way Christopher behaves as a result of his condition. For instance, the challenge of caring for Christopher evidently played a part in Mother's decision to leave, years earlier. Although this action takes place outside the story Christopher tells in the novel, we learn of it when Christopher discovers Mother's letters. She talks about how Christopher once became nervous in a crowded store, and when she tried to move him he knocked several mixers off a shelf. Mother says she left because she felt it was in Christopher's and Father's best interests, and she suggests that Christopher's behavior proved more than she could cope with. "Maybe if things had been different, maybe if you'd been differant [this is her spelling error], I might have been better at it," she writes. Mrs. Shears also apparently breaks off her relationship with Father—resulting in the anger that leads Father to kill Wellington—at least in part because Christopher's condition caused them stress. As Father explains why he murdered Wellington, he says, "I think she cared more for that bloody dog than for me, for us. And maybe that's not so stupid, looking back. Maybe we are a bloody handful . . . I mean, shit, buddy, we're not exactly low-maintenance, are we?" Christopher's condition leads more directly to his conflict with Father than it did to the conflict in these instances. Specifically, Christopher's limited understanding of other people causes him to believe Father might actually kill him, since Father at this point has already admitted to killing Wellington. Christopher runs away to London largely in response to this fear, and the conflict we see between Father and Christopher in the second half of the novel derives to a great degree from this misunderstanding of Father's motives.

Essay Topics

1.   *Christopher quotes Mother as saying that his behavior would "drive her to an early grave." Citing evidence from the text, to what extent does Christopher feel responsible for*

Mother's "death"? Do her letters and eventual reappearance change how he feels?

2.   Think of the novel as narrated in the third person, instead of by Christopher. Describe how this change would affect our views of the characters and the emotional impact of the novel.

3.   Christopher appears to believe in always acting logically. Does Christopher always behave logically, and what does this tell us about his character?

4.   Describe the significant ways in which Christopher's character has and has not changed over the course of the novel.

How to Write Literary Analysis

The Literary Essay: A Step-by-Step Guide

When you read for pleasure, your only goal is enjoyment. You might find yourself reading to get caught up in an exciting story, to learn about an interesting time or place, or just to pass time. Maybe you're looking for inspiration, guidance, or a reflection of your own life. There are as many different, valid ways of reading a book as there are books in the world.

When you read a work of literature in an English class, however, you're being asked to read in a special way: you're being asked to perform *literary analysis*. To analyze something means to break it down into smaller parts and then examine how those parts work, both individually and together. Literary analysis involves examining all the parts of a novel, play, short story, or poem—elements such as character, setting, tone, and imagery—and thinking about how the author uses those elements to create certain effects.

A literary essay isn't a book review: you're not being asked whether or not you liked a book or whether you'd recommend it to another reader. A literary essay also isn't like the kind of book report you wrote when you were younger, where your teacher wanted you to summarize the book's action. A high school or college-level literary essay asks, "How does this piece of literature actually work?" "How does it do what it does?" and, "Why might the author have made the choices he or she did?"

The Seven Steps
No one is born knowing how to analyze literature; it's a skill you learn and a process you can master. As you gain more practice with this kind of thinking and writing, you'll be able to craft a method that works best for you. But until then, here are seven basic steps to writing a well-constructed literary essay:

    1. Ask questions
    2. Collect evidence
    3. Construct a thesis

4. Develop and organize arguments
5. Write the introduction
6. Write the body paragraphs
7. Write the conclusion

---

1. ASK QUESTIONS

When you're assigned a literary essay in class, your teacher will often provide you with a list of writing prompts. Lucky you! Now all you have to do is choose one. Do yourself a favor and pick a topic that interests you. You'll have a much better (not to mention easier) time if you start off with something you enjoy thinking about. If you are asked to come up with a topic by yourself, though, you might start to feel a little panicked. Maybe you have too many ideas—or none at all. Don't worry. Take a deep breath and start by asking yourself these questions:

- **What struck you?** Did a particular image, line, or scene linger in your mind for a long time? If it fascinated you, chances are you can draw on it to write a fascinating essay.

- **What confused you?** Maybe you were surprised to see a character act in a certain way, or maybe you didn't understand why the book ended the way it did. Confusing moments in a work of literature are like a loose thread in a sweater: if you pull on it, you can unravel the entire thing. Ask yourself why the author chose to write about that character or scene the way he or she did and you might tap into some important insights about the work as a whole.

- **Did you notice any patterns?** Is there a phrase that the main character uses constantly or an image that repeats throughout the book? If you can figure out how that pattern weaves through the work and what the significance of that pattern is, you've almost got your entire essay mapped out.

- **Did you notice any contradictions or ironies?** Great works of literature are complex; great literary essays recognize and explain those complexities. Maybe the title (*Happy Days*) totally disagrees with the book's subject matter (hungry orphans dying in the woods). Maybe the main character acts one way around his family and a completely different way around his friends and associates. If you can find a way to explain a work's contradictory elements, you've got the seeds of a great essay.

At this point, you don't need to know exactly what you're going to say about your topic; you just need a place to begin your exploration. You can help direct your reading and brainstorming by formulating your topic as a *question,* which you'll then try to answer in your essay. The best questions invite critical debates and discussions, not just a rehashing of the summary. Remember, you're looking for something you can *prove or argue* based on evidence you find in the text. Finally, remember to keep the scope of your question in mind: is this a topic you can adequately address within the word or page limit you've been given? Conversely, is this a topic big enough to fill the required length?

GOOD QUESTIONS

> *"Are Romeo and Juliet's parents responsible for the deaths of their children?"*
>
> *"Why do pigs keep showing up in* LORD OF THE FLIES*?"*
>
> *"Are Dr. Frankenstein and his monster alike? How?"*

BAD QUESTIONS

> *"What happens to Scout in* TO KILL A MOCKINGBIRD*?"*
>
> *"What do the other characters in* JULIUS CAESAR *think about Caesar?"*
>
> *"How does Hester Prynne in* THE SCARLET LETTER *remind me of my sister?"*

---

2. COLLECT EVIDENCE

Once you know what question you want to answer, it's time to scour the book for things that will help you answer the question. Don't worry if you don't know what you want to say yet—right now you're just collecting ideas and material and letting it all percolate. Keep track of passages, symbols, images, or scenes that deal with your topic. Eventually, you'll start making connections between these examples and your thesis will emerge.

Here's a brief summary of the various parts that compose each and every work of literature. These are the elements that you will analyze in your essay, and which you will offer as evidence to support your arguments.

LITERARY ANALYSIS

ELEMENTS OF STORY   These are the *what*s of the work—what happens, where it happens, and to whom it happens.

- **Plot:** All of the events and actions of the work.
- **Character:** The people who act and are acted upon in a literary work. The main character of a work is known as the *protagonist*.
- **Conflict:** The central tension in the work. In most cases, the protagonist wants something, while opposing forces (antagonists) hinder the protagonist's progress.
- **Setting:** When and where the work takes place. Elements of setting include location, time period, time of day, weather, social atmosphere, and economic conditions.
- **Narrator:** The person telling the story. The narrator may straightforwardly report what happens, convey the subjective opinions and perceptions of one or more characters, or provide commentary and opinion in his or her own voice.
- **Themes:** The main idea or message of the work—usually an abstract idea about people, society, or life in general. A work may have many themes, which may be in tension with one another.

ELEMENTS OF STYLE   These are the *how*s—how the characters speak, how the story is constructed, and how language is used throughout the work.

- **Structure and organization:** How the parts of the work are assembled. Some novels are narrated in a linear, chronological fashion, while others skip around in time. Some plays follow a traditional three- or five-act structure, while others are a series of loosely connected scenes. Some authors deliberately leave gaps in their works, leaving readers to puzzle out the missing information. A work's structure and organization can tell you a lot about the kind of message it wants to convey.
- **Point of view:** The perspective from which a story is told. In *first-person point of view,* the narrator involves himself or herself in the story. ("I went to the store"; "We watched in horror as the bird slammed into the window.") A first-person narrator is usually the protagonist of the work, but not always. In *third-person point of view,* the narrator does not participate

in the story. A third-person narrator may closely follow a specific character, recounting that individual character's thoughts or experiences, or it may be what we call an *omniscient* narrator. Omniscient narrators see and know all: they can witness any event in any time or place and are privy to the inner thoughts and feelings of all characters. Remember that the narrator and the author are not the same thing!

- **Diction:** Word choice. Whether a character uses dry, clinical language or flowery prose with lots of exclamation points can tell you a lot about his or her attitude and personality.

- **Syntax:** Word order and sentence construction. Syntax is a crucial part of establishing an author's narrative voice. Ernest Hemingway, for example, is known for writing in very short, straightforward sentences, while James Joyce characteristically wrote in long, incredibly complicated lines.

- **Tone:** The mood or feeling of the text. Diction and syntax often contribute to the tone of a work. A novel written in short, clipped sentences that use small, simple words might feel brusque, cold, or matter-of-fact.

- **Imagery:** Language that appeals to the senses, representing things that can be seen, smelled, heard, tasted, or touched.

- **Figurative language:** Language that is not meant to be interpreted literally. The most common types of figurative language are *metaphors* and *similes,* which compare two unlike things in order to suggest a similarity between them— for example, "All the world's a stage," or "The moon is like a ball of green cheese." (Metaphors say one thing *is* another thing; similes claim that one thing is *like* another thing.)

---

3. CONSTRUCT A THESIS

When you've examined all the evidence you've collected and know how you want to answer the question, it's time to write your thesis statement. A *thesis* is a claim about a work of literature that needs to be supported by evidence and arguments. The thesis statement is the heart of the literary essay, and the bulk of your paper will be spent trying to prove this claim. A good thesis will be:

- **Arguable**. "*The Great Gatsby* describes New York society in the 1920s" isn't a thesis—it's a fact.

- **Provable through textual evidence**. "*Hamlet* is a confusing but ultimately very well-written play" is a weak thesis because it offers the writer's personal opinion about the book. Yes, it's arguable, but it's not a claim that can be proved or supported with examples taken from the play itself.

- **Surprising**. "Both George and Lenny change a great deal in *Of Mice and Men*" is a weak thesis because it's obvious. A really strong thesis will argue for a reading of the text that is not immediately apparent.

- **Specific.** "Dr. Frankenstein's monster tells us a lot about the human condition" is *almost* a really great thesis statement, but it's still too vague. What does the writer mean by "a lot"? *How* does the monster tell us so much about the human condition?

GOOD THESIS STATEMENTS

Question: In *Romeo and Juliet*, which is more powerful in shaping the lovers' story: fate or foolishness?

Thesis: "Though Shakespeare defines Romeo and Juliet as 'star-crossed lovers' and images of stars and planets appear throughout the play, a closer examination of that celestial imagery reveals that the stars are merely witnesses to the characters' foolish activities and not the causes themselves."

Question: How does the bell jar function as a symbol in Sylvia Plath's *The Bell Jar*?

Thesis: "A bell jar is a bell-shaped glass that has three basic uses: to hold a specimen for observation, to contain gases, and to maintain a vacuum. The bell jar appears in each of these capacities in *The Bell Jar,* Plath's semi-autobiographical novel, and each appearance marks a different stage in Esther's mental breakdown."

Question: Would Piggy in *The Lord of the Flies* make a good island leader if he were given the chance?

Thesis: "Though the intelligent, rational, and innovative Piggy has the mental characteristics of a good leader, he ultimately lacks the social skills necessary to be an effective one. Golding emphasizes this point by giving Piggy a foil in the charismatic Jack, whose magnetic personality allows him to capture and wield power effectively, if not always wisely."

4. DEVELOP AND ORGANIZE ARGUMENTS

The reasons and examples that support your thesis will form the middle paragraphs of your essay. Since you can't really write your thesis statement until you know how you'll structure your argument, you'll probably end up working on steps 3 and 4 at the same time.

There's no single method of argumentation that will work in every context. One essay prompt might ask you to compare and contrast two characters, while another asks you to trace an image through a given work of literature. These questions require different kinds of answers and therefore different kinds of arguments. Below, we'll discuss three common kinds of essay prompts and some strategies for constructing a solid, well-argued case.

TYPES OF LITERARY ESSAYS

- **Compare and contrast**

  Compare and contrast the characters of Huck and Jim in THE ADVENTURES OF HUCKLEBERRY FINN.

  Chances are you've written this kind of essay before. In an academic literary context, you'll organize your arguments the same way you would in any other class. You can either go *subject by subject* or *point by point*. In the former, you'll discuss one character first and then the second. In the latter, you'll choose several traits (attitude toward life, social status, images and metaphors associated with the character) and devote a paragraph to each. You may want to use a mix of these two approaches—for example, you may want to spend a paragraph apiece broadly sketching Huck's and Jim's personalities before transitioning into a paragraph or two describing a few key points of comparison. This can be a highly effective strategy if you want to make a counterintuitive argument—that, despite seeming to be totally different, the two characters being compared are actually similar in a very important way (or vice versa). Remember that your essay should reveal something fresh or unexpected about the text, so think beyond the obvious parallels and differences.

- **Trace**

  Choose an image—for example, birds, knives, or eyes—and trace that image throughout MACBETH.

  Sounds pretty easy, right? All you need to do is read the play, underline every appearance of a knife in *Macbeth*, and then list them in your essay in the order they appear, right? Well, not exactly. Your teacher doesn't want a simple catalog of examples. He or she wants to see you make *connections* between those examples—that's the difference between summarizing and analyzing. In the *Macbeth* example above, think about the different contexts in which knives appear in the play and to what effect. In *Macbeth*, there are real knives and imagined knives; knives that kill and knives that simply threaten. Categorize and classify your examples to give them some order. Finally, always keep the overall effect in mind. After you choose and analyze your examples, you should come to some greater understanding about the work, as well as your chosen image, symbol, or phrase's role in developing the major themes and stylistic strategies of that work.

- **Debate**

  Is the society depicted in 1984 *good for its citizens?*

  In this kind of essay, you're being asked to debate a moral, ethical, or aesthetic issue regarding the work. You might be asked to judge a character or group of characters (*Is Caesar responsible for his own demise?*) or the work itself (*Is* JANE EYRE *a feminist novel?*). For this kind of essay, there are two important points to keep in mind. First, don't simply base your arguments on your personal feelings and reactions. Every literary essay expects you to read and analyze the work, so search for evidence in the text. What do characters in *1984* have to say about the government of Oceania? What images does Orwell use that might give you a hint about his attitude toward the government? As in any debate, you also need to make sure that you define all the necessary terms before you begin to argue your case. What does it mean to be a "good" society? What makes a novel "feminist"? You should define your terms right up front, in the first paragraph after your introduction.

  Second, remember that strong literary essays make contrary and surprising arguments. Try to think outside the box. In the *1984* example above, it seems like the obvious answer would be no, the totalitarian society depicted in Orwell's novel is *not* good for its citizens. But can you think of any arguments for the opposite side? Even if your final assertion is that the novel depicts a cruel, repressive, and therefore harmful society, acknowledging and responding to the counterargument will strengthen your overall case.

5. WRITE THE INTRODUCTION

Your introduction sets up the entire essay. It's where you present your topic and articulate the particular issues and questions you'll be addressing. It's also where you, as the writer, introduce yourself to your readers. A persuasive literary essay immediately establishes its writer as a knowledgeable, authoritative figure.

An introduction can vary in length depending on the overall length of the essay, but in a traditional five-paragraph essay it should be no longer than one paragraph. However long it is, your introduction needs to:

- **Provide any necessary context.** Your introduction should situate the reader and let him or her know what to expect. What book are you discussing? Which characters? What topic will you be addressing?

- **Answer the "So what?" question.** Why is this topic important, and why is your particular position on the topic noteworthy? Ideally, your introduction should pique the reader's interest by suggesting how your argument is surprising or otherwise counterintuitive. Literary essays make unexpected connections and reveal less-than-obvious truths.

- **Present your thesis.** This usually happens at or very near the end of your introduction.

- **Indicate the shape of the essay to come.** Your reader should finish reading your introduction with a good sense of the scope of your essay as well as the path you'll take toward proving your thesis. You don't need to spell out every step, but you do need to suggest the organizational pattern you'll be using.

Your introduction should not:

- **Be vague.** Beware of the two killer words in literary analysis: *interesting* and *important*. Of course the work, question, or example is interesting and important—that's why you're writing about it!

- **Open with any grandiose assertions.** Many student readers think that beginning their essays with a flamboyant statement such as, "Since the dawn of time, writers have been fascinated with the topic of free will," makes them sound important and commanding. You know what? It actually sounds pretty amateurish.

- **Wildly praise the work.** Another typical mistake student writers make is extolling the work or author. Your teacher doesn't need to be told that "Shakespeare is perhaps the greatest writer in the English language." You can mention a work's reputation in passing—by referring to *The Adventures of Huckleberry Finn* as "Mark Twain's enduring classic," for example—but don't make a point of bringing it up unless that reputation is key to your argument.

- **Go off-topic.** Keep your introduction streamlined and to the point. Don't feel the need to throw in all kinds of bells and whistles in order to impress your reader—just get to the point as quickly as you can, without skimping on any of the required steps.

6. Write the Body Paragraphs

Once you've written your introduction, you'll take the arguments you developed in step 4 and turn them into your body paragraphs. The organization of this middle section of your essay will largely be determined by the argumentative strategy you use, but no matter how you arrange your thoughts, your body paragraphs need to do the following:

- **Begin with a strong topic sentence.** Topic sentences are like signs on a highway: they tell the reader where they are and where they're going. A good topic sentence not only alerts readers to what issue will be discussed in the following paragraph but also gives them a sense of what argument will be made *about* that issue. "Rumor and gossip play an important role in *The Crucible*" isn't a strong topic sentence because it doesn't tell us very much. "The community's constant gossiping creates an environment that allows false accusations to flourish" is a much stronger topic sentence— it not only tells us *what* the paragraph will discuss (gossip) but *how* the paragraph will discuss the topic (by showing how gossip creates a set of conditions that leads to the play's climactic action).

- **Fully and completely develop a single thought.** Don't skip around in your paragraph or try to stuff in too much material. Body paragraphs are like bricks: each individual one needs to be strong and sturdy or the entire structure will collapse. Make sure you have really proven your point before moving on to the next one.

- **Use transitions effectively.** Good literary essay writers know that each paragraph must be clearly and strongly linked to the material around it. Think of each paragraph as a response to the one that precedes it. Use transition words and phrases such as *however, similarly, on the contrary, therefore,* and *furthermore* to indicate what kind of response you're making.

---

7. WRITE THE CONCLUSION

Just as you used the introduction to ground your readers in the topic before providing your thesis, you'll use the conclusion to quickly summarize the specifics learned thus far and then hint at the broader implications of your topic. A good conclusion will:

- **Do more than simply restate the thesis.** If your thesis argued that *The Catcher in the Rye* can be read as a Christian allegory, don't simply end your essay by saying, "And that is why *The Catcher in the Rye* can be read as a Christian allegory." If you've constructed your arguments well, this kind of statement will just be redundant.

- **Synthesize the arguments, not summarize them.** Similarly, don't repeat the details of your body paragraphs in your conclusion. The reader has already read your essay, and chances are it's not so long that they've forgotten all your points by now.

- **Revisit the "So what?" question.** In your introduction, you made a case for why your topic and position are important. You should close your essay with the same sort of gesture. What do your readers know now that they didn't know before? How will that knowledge help them better appreciate or understand the work overall?

- **Move from the specific to the general.** Your essay has most likely treated a very specific element of the work—a single character, a small set of images, or a particular passage. In your conclusion, try to show how this narrow discussion has wider implications for the work overall. If your essay on *To Kill a Mockingbird* focused on the character of Boo Radley, for example, you might want to include a bit in your conclusion about how he fits into the novel's larger message about childhood, innocence, or family life.

- **Stay relevant.** Your conclusion should suggest new directions of thought, but it shouldn't be treated as an opportunity to pad your essay with all the extra, interesting ideas you came up with during your brainstorming sessions but couldn't fit into the essay proper. Don't attempt to stuff in unrelated queries or too many abstract thoughts.

- **Avoid making overblown closing statements.** A conclusion should open up your highly specific, focused discussion, but it should do so without drawing a sweeping lesson about life or human nature. Making such observations may be part of the point of reading, but it's almost always a mistake in essays, where these observations tend to sound overly dramatic or simply silly.

A+ Essay Checklist

Congratulations! If you've followed all the steps we've outlined above, you should have a solid literary essay to show for all your efforts. What if you've got your sights set on an A+? To write the kind of superlative essay that will be rewarded with a perfect grade, keep the following rubric in mind. These are the qualities that teachers expect to see in a truly A+ essay. How does yours stack up?

- ✓ Demonstrates a thorough understanding of the book
- ✓ Presents an original, compelling argument
- ✓ Thoughtfully analyzes the text's formal elements
- ✓ Uses appropriate and insightful examples
- ✓ Structures ideas in a logical and progressive order
- ✓ Demonstrates a mastery of sentence construction, transitions, grammar, spelling, and word choice

LITERARY ANALYSIS

A+ Student Essay

What role does discovery play in the novel? How does the idea of discovery tie into Christopher's personal growth?

Mark Haddon's novel is, at its heart, a mystery. In fact, it's quite literally a murder mystery at the start, as Christopher seeks to learn who killed his neighbor's dog, Wellington. But while that question is answered partway through the book, Christopher's discoveries of answers to other, more personal riddles continue to drive the novel. By the end we see that the novel has been more significantly the story of Christopher's self-discovery.

Christopher's quest to get answers appears from the very beginning of the novel: He finds Wellington dead on the neighbor's lawn and he sets out immediately to learn who was responsible. Even from that initial impetus, he quickly discovers something about himself. Though it makes him uncomfortable to talk to people, he can overcome his discomfort and do it if he needs to. It's not a very momentous discovery, but it sets a precedent for the rest of the novel as Christopher faces new personal challenges that entail struggling with the unsettling facts he learns about his mother and father. What makes these issues difficult for him, of course, is his condition. It's never specified exactly what it is, but it seems clear that he has an autism-spectrum disorder, most likely Asperger's Syndrome. That condition makes it hard for Christopher to handle emotions and just about any disruption to his sense of order. Those things are exactly what he has to contend with, however, and Christopher finds himself in the midst of a chaotic emotional puzzle that he is particularly ill-equipped to handle.

The challenges get increasingly more imposing with each new discovery. He finds out his mother and father were each having an affair, that his mother is in fact alive and his father has been lying about her death for years, and that it was his father who killed Wellington. Along the way, we watch Christopher struggle to understand and process this emotionally charged information. For example, when he discovers the first of his mother's letters to him, dated after her supposed death, he comes up with different explanations for the presence of the letters. None involve guessing that his mother is still alive, despite the fact that it's the simplest solution, and even though in discussing the principle of Occam's razor immediately beforehand he stated that the simplest solution was generally the right one. His reaction suggests he doesn't want to see the truth, which is emotionally quite messy and complex, because it makes him uncomfortable. Not long after, he has no choice but to see the truth when he reads the rest of his mother's letters, and it's so overwhelming for him that he blacks out.

The rest of the novel centers on Christopher coming to terms with these revelations, which set him on a new journey. No longer trusting his father, he travels to London by himself, and the crowded, chaotic train station he must navigate parallels the emotional disorder he struggles to deal with. It's a climactic moment in the novel. The psychological toll of both is overwhelming, largely because of his condition, and he becomes nearly paralyzed by his distress. But he manages to persevere and surmount the incredible discomfort and confusion he feels.

At the end of the novel, Christopher feels proud of himself for having learned the truth about Wellington's death and overcoming all the hardships that followed. Because he was able to deal with them, he feels certain he is capable of attending a university in another town and being on his own. It's clear at this point that the true focus of the story is Christopher's remarkable personal growth, with the discoveries about Wellington's murder and about his parents serving as the challenges he had to overcome to achieve it.

LITERARY ANALYSIS

GLOSSARY OF LITERARY TERMS

ANTAGONIST

> The entity that acts to frustrate the goals of the *protagonist*. The antagonist is usually another *character* but may also be a non-human force.

ANTIHERO / ANTIHEROINE

> A *protagonist* who is not admirable or who challenges notions of what should be considered admirable.

CHARACTER

> A person, animal, or any other thing with a personality that appears in a *narrative*.

CLIMAX

> The moment of greatest intensity in a text or the major turning point in the *plot*.

CONFLICT

> The central struggle that moves the *plot* forward. The conflict can be the *protagonist*'s struggle against fate, nature, society, or another person.

FIRST-PERSON POINT OF VIEW

> A literary style in which the *narrator* tells the story from his or her own *point of view* and refers to himself or herself as "I." The narrator may be an active participant in the story or just an observer.

HERO / HEROINE

> The principal *character* in a literary work or *narrative*.

IMAGERY

> Language that brings to mind sense-impressions, representing things that can be seen, smelled, heard, tasted, or touched.

MOTIF

> A recurring idea, structure, contrast, or device that develops or informs the major *themes* of a work of literature.

NARRATIVE

> A story.

LITERARY ANALYSIS

NARRATOR

The person (sometimes a *character*) who tells a story; the *voice* assumed by the writer. The narrator and the author of the work of literature are not the same person.

PLOT

The arrangement of the events in a story, including the sequence in which they are told, the relative emphasis they are given, and the causal connections between events.

POINT OF VIEW

The *perspective* that a *narrative* takes toward the events it describes.

PROTAGONIST

The main *character* around whom the story revolves.

SETTING

The location of a *narrative* in time and space. Setting creates mood or atmosphere.

SUBPLOT

A secondary *plot* that is of less importance to the overall story but may serve as a point of contrast or comparison to the main plot.

SYMBOL

An object, *character,* figure, or color that is used to represent an abstract idea or concept. Unlike an *emblem,* a symbol may have different meanings in different contexts.

SYNTAX

The way the words in a piece of writing are put together to form lines, phrases, or clauses; the basic structure of a piece of writing.

THEME

A fundamental and universal idea explored in a literary work.

TONE

The author's attitude toward the subject or *characters* of a story or poem or toward the reader.

VOICE

An author's individual way of using language to reflect his or her own personality and attitudes. An author communicates voice through *tone, diction,* and *syntax.*

LITERARY ANALYSIS

A Note on Plagiarism

Plagiarism—presenting someone else's work as your own—rears its ugly head in many forms. Many students know that copying text without citing it is unacceptable. But some don't realize that even if you're not quoting directly, but instead are paraphrasing or summarizing, *it is plagiarism* unless you cite the source.

Here are the most common forms of plagiarism:

- Using an author's phrases, sentences, or paragraphs without citing the source
- Paraphrasing an author's ideas without citing the source
- Passing off another student's work as your own

How do you steer clear of plagiarism? You should *always* acknowledge all words and ideas that aren't your own by using quotation marks around verbatim text or citations like footnotes and endnotes to note another writer's ideas. For more information on how to give credit when credit is due, ask your teacher for guidance or visit www.sparknotes.com.

LITERARY ANALYSIS

REVIEW & RESOURCES

QUIZ

1. Wellington, which Christopher discovers dead at the outset of the novel, is what kind of animal?

   A. Poodle
   B. Tabby cat
   C. Parakeet
   D. Friend from school

2. What implement was used to kill Wellington?

   A. Swiss Army knife
   B. Shovel
   C. Garden fork
   D. Poisoned Twinkie

3. Why does the police officer arrest Christopher at the murder scene?

   A. Christopher hits the police officer
   B. Christopher is trespassing on Mrs. Shears's property
   C. Christopher has been reported missing
   D. Christopher is a suspect in the crime

4. How do Father and Mother express to Christopher that they love him?

   A. Hugging him close
   B. Spreading their fingers apart in a fan
   C. Verbally mouthing "I love you"
   D. Giving him Milkybars

5. According to Christopher's system, what kind of day will it be if Christopher sees four yellow cars in a row?

  A. Good Day
  B. Super Good Day
  C. Snow Day
  D. Black Day

6. What would Christopher like to be at the start of the book?

  A. An architect
  B. An artist
  C. An astronaut
  D. An alchemist

7. What does Christopher use to label the book's chapters?

  A. Roman numerals
  B. Cardinal numbers
  C. Morse code
  D. Prime numbers

8. What does Christopher want to be the first at his school to accomplish?

  A. Ace the A-level math exam
  B. Swim the English Channel
  C. Visit Madagascar
  D. Play Romania in football

9. What genre does Christopher label his book as?

  A. Children's book
  B. Murder mystery
  C. Romance novel
  D. Text book

10. Who is Siobhan?

  A. Christopher's teacher at school
  B. Father's coworker
  C. Christopher's invigilator
  D. Mother's maiden name

11.   What is Christopher's favorite book?

    A.   *The Masqueraders* by Georgette Heyer
    B.   *The Hound of the Baskervilles* by Sir Arthur Conan Doyle
    C.   *Dune* by Frank Herbert
    D.   *Heart of Darkness* by Joseph Conrad

12.   What does *The Case of the Cottingley Fairies* refer to?

    A.   Christopher's first novel
    B.   One of Christopher's favorite math problems
    C.   A 1917 incident involving a series of fake photographs
    D.   A collection of stories by Sir Arthur Conan Doyle

13.   Which colors does Christopher dislike?

    A.   Red and blue
    B.   Pink and purple
    C.   Yellow and brown
    D.   Green and black

14.   What concept does the Monty Hall problem demonstrate?

    A.   Intuition can be wrong
    B.   An infinite number of prime numbers exist
    C.   Goats are more valuable than cars
    D.   Wellington's murderer was male

15.   To what does Christopher compare his memory?

    A.   Trash compactor
    B.   Space shuttle
    C.   DVD player
    D.   Red car

16.   Where does Father take Christopher to apologize for their fight?

    A.   Willesden Junction
    B.   Shakespeare's Globe Theatre
    C.   Grimpen Mire
    D.   Twycross Zoo

17. Who is Toby?

    A.   Christopher's best friend at school
    B.   Christopher's pet rat
    C.   Christopher's Swiss Army knife
    D.   Christopher's uncle

18. Where does Christopher find the letters from Mother?

    A.   The mailbox
    B.   Father's shirt box
    C.   His special food box
    D.   The garden shed

19. How does Christopher define love?

    A.   Helping someone when they get into trouble and always telling that person the truth
    B.   Getting the third-degree
    C.   As a picture on the screen in our heads
    D.   Having sex with someone

20. Where does Christopher spend the night after Father confesses to killing Wellington?

    A.   At Mrs. Alexander's house
    B.   In Father's closet
    C.   Behind the garden shed
    D.   In one of the kitchen cabinets

21. Which of the following is not a logic puzzle, concept, or rule mentioned in the novel?

    A.   The Monty Hall Problem
    B.   Occam's razor
    C.   Conway's Soldiers
    D.   Train to London

REVIEW & RESOURCES

22. From sight, Christopher would be able to recognize which of the following facial expressions?

   A.   Nervous
   B.   Surprised
   C.   Jealous
   D.   Sad

23. At the end of the novel, what does Father give to Christopher?

   A.   A hug
   B.   The keys to his van
   C.   A puppy
   D.   The book he took from Christopher

24. Which of the following characters is alive at the end of the novel?

   A.   Wellington
   B.   Mother
   C.   Toby
   D.   Mr. Paulson

25. At the end of the novel, Christopher is hopeful for the future for all but which of the following reasons?

   A.   Because he went to London on his own
   B.   Because he solved Wellington's murder
   C.   Because he wrote a book
   D.   Because he has gotten into university

ANSWER KEY

1: A; 2: C; 3: A; 4: B; 5: D; 6: C; 7: D; 8: A; 9: B; 10: A; 11: B; 12: C;
13: C; 14: A; 15: C; 16: D; 17: B; 18: B; 19: A; 20: C; 21: D; 22: D;
23: C; 24: B; 25: D